REALITY

by

Michael Featherstone. BA (Hons) Fine Art. 2020

REALITY

First Edition

Copyright Michael Featherstone 2021

Published by Amazon UK

Thanks to all of the friends, authors, mediums and researchers whose work has played a large part in the foundation of this book though they won't all necessarily agree with my ideas. Thanks also to my family for putting up with my obsession with the never-ending book.

Mike Featherstone, BA (Hons.) Fine Art. February 2021

CONTENTS

IN THE BEGINING.

Humanity's deepest desire for knowledge is justification enough for our continuing quest and our goal is nothing less than a complete description of the universe we live in.

(Stephen Hawking.)

Human beings need hope, some certainty that everything they achieve and experience will not be wasted and that their beliefs have some foundation in reality. Are we like insects that live for a day, then gone, as if we never existed or, are we eternal beings with endless potential to love, to create and to explore? There's a saying, 'What you see is what you get', but when you look at the world in a purely scientific way that is not strictly true, it is more strange than Alice's Wonderland and no less weird than anything we might image a heavenly world to be.

All of us took the world for granted until we saw the first images from space then suddenly we realized the vulnerability of this beautiful orb on which we live; man alone in a vast universe. Imagine that we can see the whole history of the earth, not in millions of years but in minutes: Visualize that bleak and barren landscape. - In the depths of the ocean something stirs, in seconds a creature appears making its way on to the land and before your eyes you see it change shape many times. Like the trick photography where Mr. Hyde is changing back into Doctor Jekyll, the creature gradually changes into the human being we know today. Just like television's 'Morph,' the little man who sprouts from a lump of plasticine, a living thing has emerged from the dead earth; the human body with its infinitely complex systems for movement and calculations: A machine that has self-awareness clinging to the side of this huge rock, whirling through space, one amongst an infinite number, suspended for an unimaginable length of time in a seemingly endless universe. Here and there is an inferno of heat, a provider of light and energy, and all the while earth's temperature stays within strict limits bringing us every season from the dead of winter to the hot summer sun. The earth, like a sophisticated laboratory, has given birth to, and supported, life in such a complicated way that it is impossible to imagine as we look at ourselves, the countless centuries of evolution that have brought about the human body; a highly complex machine; so beautiful to look at and the vehicle for our consciousness; the personality; the face we love; evolved step by step; year by year from tiny organisms in the primeval soup. Through studying nature we become acutely aware of the oddities of life in all of its many and varied forms. Each has its own ingenious way of existing and all are set in a balance to sustain one another to be a part of the beautiful and ever-changing picture, which is the earth in all its glory. Nothing is wasted, everything fits into the picture so neatly; take for instance the water cycle. The nourishing rivers and streams fill the seas, then through evaporation, form the clouds which paint our beautiful skies and provide us with refreshing, and life-giving rain returning once again to those same rivers from whence it came. - The same rain that fell on the Dinosaur falls on us today. Forensic scientist Patricia Wiltshire used to tell her students, '*A molecule in your eye could have been part of a dinosaur's toe.*'

(Patricia Wiltshire. 'Life Scientific' BBC Radio 4. Tues Jan 7th 2020.)

Every living creature is a work of art, an example to science and technology; one of the most amazing birds I saw recently on TV was the bird of paradise which first of all tidies the stage removing every leaf, every piece of clutter then engages in a complicated dance with the ability to change eye colour and spin like a whirling dervish to attract a mate. Some animals and birds show a remarkable ability to solve problems that would perplex any human child and their emotional reactions for example to death can also be like ours. Washoe the chimp could even use sign language and abstract reasoning, many creatures use clicks or whistles to communicate with each other whilst horses rub noses and bees dance. More recently David Attenborough has shown us the most remarkable forms of life in the deep, deep oceans with creatures displaying flashing fairy lights, transparent or grotesque bodies the like of which have been the inspiration for horror films, and evidence of using reason and logic to prevent being eaten. Even relatively simple organisms like plants are not without plenty of clever tricks: Some have D.I.Y skills; others are masters of disguise and there are a huge variety of defence mechanisms, from stings and poisons, to suits of armour. Consider the flowers sprouting out of the ground, they do credit to any designer, only their familiarity fools us into forgetting how strange this phenomenon is. If we stood before a bare patch of soil and watched a beautiful garden appear within seconds, we would be amazed and yet because we do not actually see flowers grow we take them for granted. Watching the time-release cameras reveal the growing patterns of the various trees and plants and the evolution of such beautiful landscapes is like seeing the set of some lavish West-End Stage production blossom by itself. Like the automatic switches in our buildings that open doors, adjust the heating and the lights the activity of so many things in nature are triggered by light, heat or pressure. Plants are full of technical wizardry much of which we cannot yet match: There are those, which explode like the squirting cucumber, others have seeds that fall to the ground like a helicopter such as the sycamore or the Tri-Star plant, with its six blades. There are gliders and there is jet propulsion whilst some seeds swim or hitch a ride. Alongside these is an abundance of food with every kind of medicine, all there for the taking and even the waste is not wasted. It's as though some mad inventor were poking fun at our so-called intelligence.

Tomato and tobacco plants and some cacti make sounds, at frequencies humans cannot hear, when they are stressed by a lack of water or having their stem cut. Microphones placed 10 centimetres from the plants picked up sounds in the ultrasonic range of 20 to 100 kilohertz, which the researchers say insects and some mammals would be capable of hearing and responding to from up to 5 metres away. A moth may decide against laying eggs on a plant that sounds water-stressed, they speculate. It is even possible to distinguish between the sounds to know what the stress is. ('Squealing plants' 'New Scientist.' 2019.)

Everything is in perfect order; everything is in its place but imagine if flowers sprouted eyes and watched you admiring them or if Elephants could speak. Humans could have had the head of a crocodile or the neck of a Giraffe, they could have been born with two heads or eight legs but they weren't, though undoubtedly the process can go tragically wrong. We marvel at the aeroplane whilst a bumblebee buzzes by hardly noticed, a small, heavier-than-air machine with the gift of free will. Should we be happy to accept that the world as we see it now came about by trial and error alone? Consider the tree, the reverse of our lungs, was it designed as part of our life support system or to add beauty to the earth? - Perhaps after all it was simply responding to its environment. How would we feel if a tree uprooted and walked away, an object that in human terms is dead, grown from dead matter, suddenly becoming alive before our eyes? Of course a tree was never designed to do that but the human being was, why should the dead earth give birth to a living, thinking creature that can become separate and move about where it will and is able to know that the mighty universe exists?

A human being is a complicated machine and whilst it takes a factory full of skilled men to build a comparatively simple motorcar, the body builds itself, changes its size and replaces every cell so that over a period of time nothing of the original is left. It mends its own punctures and reproduces itself; the nerves are wired like a telephone exchange; the immune system operates like a video game and the skeleton is a mechanical marvel. Even the simple act of walking was not duplicated by a machine until 1997, and this was only achieved by using very complicated engineering and electronics. This sausage on legs, this walking bag of bones and chemicals, is controlled by the brain, a highly advanced computer. (Or an intelligent cauliflower!) The camera impresses us but we take for granted our eyes grown like fruit on a bush; there is even a television picture inside our heads. And all of this was already in existence when dinosaurs roamed the earth many millions of years before television was even thought of. The sheer sophistication of so-called primitive animals came home to me as I saw the immense speed and skill with which a big cat chased it prey.

There are faces we may hate and faces we undoubtedly love but that face, which so represents our individuality, is composed of functional gadgets just like any motorcar. Science could not even imagine inventing a face which can sculpt itself from the inside out. The eyes are to see with, the nose and mouth to breathe in the gases to keep us alive in this bubble of air that surrounds us. The mouth takes in fuel and like the ears is part of the communications system so that we can share our thoughts with each other. The body is a vehicle in which we drive around and we can love a car pretty much in the way that we can love a face. Its appearance may attract us but the human face becomes inseparable from the personality. The Disney artists are masters at making objects appear life-like, the candlesticks, the tea cups, the milk jug are all endowed with their own personality, just like the human body, a sophisticated puppet, an object brought to life but by what? Perhaps we are after all just clever machines, a race of robots living in a macabre fantasy world sprung up from the dead earth and clinging to every second of life, before we return to a terrible life-less eternity. If that were true, all the dreaming, all the hoping, all the theories and all the faith in the world would not make it otherwise.

Scientists think they understand the mechanics of evolution but in its way the human body, this complex bag of tricks that has appeared as it were from nowhere, is as strange a phenomena as if a block of flats had sprouted out of the ground complete with electrical wiring, plumbing and working lifts, which then grew bigger and bigger for some eighteen years or so until it reached full size. If it were ever to happen then no doubt the scientists would be able to understand how it came about, and after a long period of time would cease to regard it as strange but we would have to ask where the technology came from that brought such a thing into being. Everything in life appears to part of one vast design, even the separate parts of an infectious virus assemble themselves in a way that reminds me of Christmas' past when I used to have to put together the kid's plastic toys or games. Oddly enough I noticed that the Open University programme, which featured this phenomenon showed the film of an exploded block of flats played backwards so that the millions of fragments came back together to form the finished product. - We are asked to believe that the human body came about by trial and error alone, anyone who cannot see that is treated as a fool though admittedly the alternative explanation is even more fantastical. It may be possible to show how certain elements reacted with each other in a long chain of events until life was formed but the individual building blocks would have no conscious plan to work to. For instance, the nerves from the eye find their way to the new brain following a train of chemical reactions. Perhaps the genes are evidence of the skill of the programmer and evolution just a story of the mechanics of it all rather than an understanding of the why of it: When I look at a human being I see technology which is so clever, so far in advance of anything we could ever dream of creating including the energy which keeps living things relentlessly on the move surpassing any battery ever made by man.

At a domino rally each piece has been carefully placed so that on the big day the effects will be produced which the designer had in mind. One simple domino falling over produces such a variety of patterns, step by step, one by one and like evolution itself successful designs flourish in the right environment whilst unsuccessful ones fail. Maybe there is a designer, a mind or minds actively involved in its development or perhaps it was all planned in the beginning like a huge computer program, or a video game where even apparently random events are accounted for? The flower may be showing us the true story of creation: Like an app. there in the seed or bulb are all the ingredients to produce the final effect just as the primeval soup contained everything necessary to create life in all its forms. Suppose that a camera has captured those earthly scenes from the very beginning and that you are now watching a speeded up version of the final film. - See how the whole planet blossoms like a flower.

How the universe, together with the earth and all that lives upon it, came to be in the first place is beyond belief. Mankind is like a man from some lost tribe who has wandered into a car factory, there he sees the robots busily working away like living things, he knows nothing of electricity or of motorcars and only understands it in terms of his own upbringing. To him it would be a place of wonders, of gods and spirits and for centuries man has looked at the universe in that same primitive light. He now prides himself that he knows better, he knows that the universe wasn't created after all, it simply evolved. By the same token he has unwittingly rejected the knowledge of our ancestors as the basic facts have been lost midst man's imaginings. Scientists may be brilliant in their own field but when it comes to this subject they simply have an opinion whilst those scientists who are researching survival are seen as eccentric. What some say in public is very different from what they say in private and we simple-minded folks can make fundamental errors in our reasoning because we don't know enough about the subject. On the other hand the common man has a kind of rough and ready wisdom that often escapes the more knowledgeable and some things are so obvious they defy explanation. What we have to remember is that scientists are discovering what is already there and they can't even make a worm or a blade of grass: In other words there is an intelligence that is infinitely greater than theirs and yet some people are happy to credit that intelligence to mere chance. In years gone by men talked of the 'creation' as though they could see the hand of God in the world: the artist, the designer, the planner, the creator. To the modern mind very much concerned with the nuts and bolts of the thing, that appears to be childish and ignorant, God is imagined as an old man, a magician who makes things appear with a wave of a magic wand: How much more reasonable to believe that the universe, our world, our beautiful landscapes, created themselves by trial and error. But why should matter create anything that is so organized? Throw a few colours on to a palette and mix them up the chances are you will end up with a muddy brown; to create a picture of beauty requires skill and experience. According to Professors Hoyle and Wickramsinghe:-

"Once we see that the probability of life, originating at random is so utterly minuscule as to make it absurd, it becomes sensible to think that the favourable properties of physics on which life depends are in every respect deliberate ." (Hoyle / Wickramsinghe 'Evolution from Space.' Dent. 1991.)

However these two professors looked for their answer in outer space which throws up the same problems. Reading about the very beginnings of the universe I wonder how such a highly complex system of gasses, forces and electronic particles appeared so quickly. Also we don't know whether the big bang was merely an event that marked a change with all of that energy being poured forth from some other pre-existing dimension. - Maybe universes live and die like everything else in an endless chain.

The idea of a heaven above might seem to be a childish belief, a simple idea for simple minds but is our familiarity with this world blinding us to the obvious? As science has a greater effect on our daily lives most of us try to reason things out rather than resorting to simple beliefs or superstitions that may be a long way from the truth. We construct within our minds a model of how we think things are, the danger being that something we have believed in has been proved untrue, because all of the facts were not at our disposal. In medicine, for example, old ideas have sometimes been turned completely on their head: what was wrong becomes right and what was right becomes wrong, it may even boil down to a different perception of those same facts. Ask someone to make four equal-sided triangles with six matches and he or she will probably lay them out on the table then find that no amount of juggling makes this possible. When three of the matches form a triangle flat on the table, and the other three are made to stand up in the shape of a three sided pyramid, the problem is solved - a three-dimensional answer to what appeared to be a two dimensional problem. And so it is with any system or belief, it is a working theory until new discoveries are made: It doesn't pay to be too dogmatic about what we think we know. Despite all of the impressive evidence, the following picture that unfolds will seem like an unbelievable fantasy but just a few decades ago the wonders of the age in which we now live were unimaginable and would have sounded just as fantastic: That carts and carriages would move on their own and the suggestion that we could see and hear people on the other side of the earth might have got you burned at the stake; now satellite television is part of everyday life. The man who suggested that Africa was once joined to America and that whole continents were on the move was laughed at and it was not until the nineteen sixties that this seemingly crazy idea was taken seriously. A beam of light can cut metal or send millions of messages whilst computers that can complete endless hours of calculations in seconds and once filled a whole room can now be held in the palm of the hand. No one could have foreseen that there would ever be a moment when a mother would put her hand upon the chest of a stranger and feel her son's heart beating or that someone could eat his breakfast with another man's hand. Men have travelled to the moon and walked in space and have seen into the far distance of the seemingly endless universe. The list of wonders grows every day and there are bound to be things that we have yet to imagine because mankind will keep on inventing and discovering therefore the world of the future is sure to be even more fantastic. The universe is based on electronic principles and in a few short years we have seen what can be done using electronics – I think we will find that almost anything is possible! Even though science is relatively speaking at the beginning of its journey scientific fact and fiction are demonstrating how clever and how truly amazing designers and inventors can be in all kinds of areas; perhaps one day even Android Robots will become part of everyday life; a thought which I find incredibly spooky but will they be alive? And so one of the underlying aims of this book is to consider the feasibility of surviving death and all that it means but in an evidential way rather than by belief alone.

But surely the whole idea of a life-after-death is religious nonsense, born of superstition and legend which has come from the imagination of very primitive people. We've seen people up mountains waiting for the world to end and brainwashed individuals prepared to die, or kill others, for their beliefs. - All of them declared that they had the proof and that everyone else was wrong. Most of us feel rather superior to these 'simple-minded' people, but the evidence suggests that we are as much victims of our outlook as they are for we are inclined to assume certain things are impossible simply because we do not understand how they might work. I once remember being on a jury listening to the prosecution and thinking what a waste of time and money it all was; the man in the dock was obviously guilty: If I hadn't been forced to sit and listen to the defence I would never have understood the other side of the argument. There is an old proverb that begins; *'The wise man doubts often and changes his mind...'*

BEINGS OF LIGHT.

Though complex and wonderful this grand design may be, from another point of view our existence seems like a science fiction story. I want you to use your imagination and see that in scientific terms every single thing in the universe is an illusion, and that other possibilities are not so farfetched in comparison. Much of what we object to in any idea of existing after death is because we think of solid objects in a solid universe like the person who looks at his TV and imagines post cards flying through the air and onto the screen. He is totally unaware of the series of codes that rebuild the picture and which produces the image of the newsreader in front of him and the same can be said of our sight. There are over thirty parts of the brain dedicated to recognizing different aspects of what we are looking at which begs the question, what is it that is doing the actual seeing. First we must consider the building blocks of everything that exists: Within the world of solid things; of wood and stone; of walls, glass and carpets; of trees and flowers; of people and objects, is another world, the world of the atom. Like the mighty planets they too are suspended in space, everyone and everything is composed of these tiny electrical charges, we ourselves are beings made of light living in a sea of light. The room, the house, and indeed the whole universe are virtually made out of nothing: Just concentrate on an object before you and try to imagine that. Why, in this cloudy dream-like world should dense clusters of atoms form complex shapes; a human being; a table; a chair? Radio and television signals drift through almost unaware of these so-called solid objects for this life of shadows is based on electronic principles. According to physicists 98% of the matter within the universe is invisible -the so called dark energy, dark matter: - Perhaps the universe is suspended in an invisible *electronic matrix* which controls, affects or arranges all heavenly bodies for example through gravity. Some physicists are talking about String Theory, presumably other physical dimensions in which life might exist in all sorts of weird and wonderful forms and if mind can be shown to be a separate entity to the body, if it can leave the body and live in other realities then maybe we have our heavens. The universe is made from light energy like a ghost or a *virtual creation; a program; a digital cloud,* suspended in space like a TV channel or a computer file, perhaps one alongside countless others of infinite variety. Historically in mystical terms these different worlds and the people who live there are referred to as being on different vibrations which we now understand are like the signals which carry television stations, invisible yet all around and about us and totally independent of each other. A ghost is solid and real in his or her own state and whilst they may see *us* as ghosts they cannot see people on a higher vibration.

This world of ours is filled with a seemingly endless number of living things each exploring a different way of existing from the weird microscopic creatures that live on our faces to strange alien-like beings at the bottom of the deepest oceans. That variety extends into the atomic world that is composed of numerous particles with strange sounding names including matter that can pass through matter and particles that some *claim* can affect each other when not even connected: And like Dr Who's '*Weeping angels*' atoms won't move while you watch.

(The Zeno Effect.) (In Our Time, BBC Radio 4. 22nd Sept 2016.)

Even time is not sacred to these tiny building blocks of the Universe.

"When an atom wants to evolve it throws out probability waves into the future to test which way things are going in much the same way that we throw out thoughts."

('Start the Week.' BBC Radio 4. May 96.)

Most people are used to the idea of talking, moving pictures in the corner of the room but imagine a time traveller has just arrived from Victorian England. He sees the life-like image of the news reader on the TV, a matrix of coloured dots, an illusion and he compares it with what he knows;

the magic lantern. You take the back off the Television and show him the printed circuit board with its tiny components and explain that at this very moment the newsreader is actually reading the news in a studio in London many miles away. You point to a microchip, a black piece of plastic with some silver wires coming out of it but without months of intensive study, how could our time traveller appreciate the many steps of discovery, of hard work and research that have lead to the creation of this electronic marvel? The same can be said of the human body and it's long journey of evolution; very real in the physical sense but in another way no more real than that image of the newsreader on the screen, it is a three-dimensional shadow, or what one physicist calls, "Animated Stardust." We are electronic ghosts in an electronic universe we exist in a kind of digital cloud.

Reality emerges from information, leading to the dramatic conclusion: the whole universe is an entangled web of quantum bits. (Physicist Vlatko Vedral. New scientist May 2020.)

The human body then is not a solid object it isn't like Lego but living beings have some other element to give them life, man may call it the eternal soul but where did that idea come from?

Looking for answers to the big questions is always going to throw up contradictions and scenarios that are hard to visualise or indeed come to terms with. Every day now new discoveries in science are changing our world in a way we couldn't envisage even a year or so ago, science fiction is becoming science fact and common sense can no longer be our guide to a future which is round the bend and out of sight.

POINTS OF VIEW.

In my previous incarnation, that is before I retired, I was a Television Engineer: I had to understand how the equipment worked before I could find the fault therefore I look at the world around me and I want to know how and why. I am looking at both science and psychic science to see what they tell us about our reality: There are so many theories, legends, tall stories and religions that to claim that I am the only sane person in the mad house is futile however; any thinking person should at least consider the following remarkable events that stand out from the everyday and which shed light on the origins and reasons for our existence. Personally I find these questions deeply interesting and I would imagine that most people have thought about them at some time or other but this subject does fire up strong emotions as if any attempt to understand them will offend our reason. This means that certain facts are continuously dismissed as farcical and nothing is learned. There are way-out theories about many subjects and often they are very convincing as they weave together incredible coincidences with a plethora of misinformation, no wonder people are sceptical. This book is food for thought; it attempts to present a different view of reality and our place in the scheme of things. I want it to be seen as a fact finding tour though I make no apologies for adding a little hearsay and conjecture and anything else which might help us to at least try to imagine the bigger picture. The mere existence of the universe and everything in it is truly preposterous. Here we are on a tiny globe, a desert island in seemingly endless space. In one short period of time we live out our lives; achieve great things; take part in all kinds of dramas and learn so much but despite our cleverness, one day we cease to exist like a light bulb that goes pop and is thrown in the bin: Our relationships become mere memories and even they fade in a relatively short time. For many a belief that they will live on in another place where life is perfect, gives comfort and hope whilst for the rest that thinking is primitive, not true, not technically feasible and quite frankly ridiculous as when the brain dies the personality ceases to exist: But! How did consciousness and such immense complexity which is our reality come into what appears to be a dead mechanical universe? Some of the events in this volume certainly make ones head spin but I think it's important to know that they really do exist. There are plenty of sceptics to support the opposite arguments however it seems to me that they are expressing opinion as fact rather than firsthand knowledge: But I would say that wouldn't I? I don't blame them for being sceptical however the truth is that evidence is widespread and proof is not as uncommon as is believed. Much of the very interesting material is coming from ordinary people the world over who claim to have witnessed alternative realities either when they have left the body during a near-death experience or because it has always been a natural ability: Some events happen only once in a lifetime. We need to know if survival of death is feasible, if there is hard evidence, and what it all means. I have had 48 years learning to understand how evidence is obtained through personal friends; the general public; a vast amount of reading and my own experience as a non psychic. They say that 'seeing is believing' of course that's not necessarily true but reminiscing recently about a particular experience which I will come to later, my son made the comment 'If you weren't my dad I would say that you were barking mad.' The hard fact is that my proof is not proof to anyone else. I want to simplify what is a very complicated and fascinating subject therefore it is not my intention to go too deeply into the question of evidence in this volume' More is contained in my unpublished work *'The Living Dream'* which has become the foundation of this book. Proof and evidence are not the same thing however what I am interested in is what the *'other side'* have to say about the greater reality of both their world and ours. I won't be dredging through the quagmire of religious beliefs most of which are different versions of the same thing containing a certain amount of fact mixed with all kinds of fables, misinterpretations and assumptions. The primary view of religion is that it has caused more death and destruction than anything else; on the other hand those religious people who are the good guys are seen as naive and simple minded: The inspirational philosophy together with the goodness and kindness that people do got lost in the middle of it all. Religion is like a suit of clothes a personal choice and usually part of one's culture. It is basically about being a good person, believing in God and being part of a supportive community but when it is used as an excuse to commit unkind or cruel acts it is patently not true to its founder's beliefs. That is why we need to look beyond faith-based reasoning at logical research and practical real-life events in the light of current knowledge. Seen in context it becomes more logical, more understandable and perhaps more believable, it has a force all of its own which is greater than some of its individual parts. The fact is that the whole world is dying and everyone pretends it isn't happening as if grandmas, grandpas, mums, dads and kids are being hoarded into cattle trucks and sent off to some unknown destination whilst everyone looks the other way. Until Charles Darwin published his book 'The Origin of the Species.' mankind's outlook was probably based on dreams; events in nature; imagination; an altered state of consciousness; the writings of various prophets and the teachings of spiritual masters that men have called Gods. Even the sun the moon and the stars would be mysterious or intimidating and it would seem that more people did claim to see all kinds of spirits when life was simpler especially in the landscape; there seems to have been a lot of fear about 'evil' and troublesome spirits then. Until relatively recently the next world with its angels, saints and vengeful Gods were very much part of daily life and still is in many parts of the world. In only a very short time evidence-based research created the technological world we have today. At the forefront of that change were some of the same scientists that investigated mediums when séances became the latest craze. During these early years groups were formed calling themselves Spiritualists; now the thought that this might take us back to yet another weird religion is perhaps a barrier to many who would dearly like some answers to the big questions. It is however one of the very rich sources of evidence as sensitives gravitate to a place where others can empathise with what they are experiencing and will want to know that it is true. They need to learn how to speak in public as passing on information without unintentionally altering the meaning is not an easy task and misunderstandings can have damaging consequences. The lesser known side of mediumship is inspirational philosophy from which we can hopefully find answers to our questions though this too can be distorted by the medium's mind which has an opinion of its own.

Not so long ago things that were thought of as being possible only in the realms of mystery and magic are now a part of everyday life. We can't imagine what might be discovered in the future but even then these changes are likely to be a far cry from our understanding of the greater reality. Whilst the scientific community in general *seem* to be atheists a U.K. survey of 2,060 people in 2008 showed 53 per cent believe in life after death, 55 per cent believe in heaven and 70 per cent believe in the human soul: (The Telegraph.) Are we then stuck with belief or is there anything more tangible that we can get our teeth into? In a personal sense everyone's life is their own reality: I call it living in a bubble which can contain all kinds of daily activities, interests, beliefs and now social media which I think for many is often an attempt to shut out the true reality of one's own situation in life: Sceptics too have constructed such a strong belief that life after death is a fantasy that their bubble is not for bursting. Our outlook isn't always a life-style choice however and can differ wildly according to life's experiences; wealth; health; poverty; natural disasters; bereavement; divorce; accident; unemployment; war and just growing older. After any traumatic change one wonders can this really be happening to me? Some people actually missed the challenge of war and one dissident said that life seemed empty after the coming of Glasnost under the Soviets. A different point of view, a change of opinion can be no less dramatic for instance; belief; non belief; depression; a feeling of pointlessness; fear even: Then there is the danger of escapism through drugs or drink. Our personal reality is who we are, it is how we relate to the world, to life and we won't change our viewpoint for all the tea in China; that is until we do and it isn't always for the worst. Expectations change, there are suddenly different priorities, and minds do alter. Sometimes it's as if the mould of our lives needs to be broken, perhaps there is something else we need to know and the script needs to be rewritten. Often very negative lives can turn into positive ones: I remember watching 'The Time and the Place' (ITV) People had gone through all kinds of horrific things and found that their lives have been transformed by new interests and experiences. Some had survived a life-threatening illness and found that every new day had a special meaning. For many there are plenty of joyful experiences but sadly some people live their lives without hope or purpose; perhaps an examination of the facts can make them think again. I believe that at the end of life on earth we will realise the caring that there is for every one of us and the tremendous value of a life lived as a human being whatever kind of life that was.

It costs us nothing to dream and it's exciting to imagine the impossible after all this has resulted in ground-breaking fiction which turned into important scientific discoveries however, just because something sounds like a good idea, or we want it to be true, it doesn't necessarily make it so. It is essential that we see the whole picture especially in a broad subject like this. It can be great fun to speculate on such big questions as; what is consciousness; how did the universe come into being; and who made God etc. Sadly there is a rule in polite circles 'Never discuss religion and politics,' that means a lot of informative and interesting experiences are hidden away for fear of ridicule: Its facts versus opinion but facts that sound like the ravings of a madman. Whenever I talked about my book individuals told me things that they couldn't even tell their own family. The claim that we survive death can be met with a lot of scorn and name calling but to be fair it is frustrating for most people not to be able to see any evidence for themselves. Listening to views on a wide range of topics on for example radio phone-ins, particularly listeners with expertise or firsthand knowledge, demonstrate that what we think about most subjects is greatly over simplified; but that doesn't stop us from having an opinion anyway so we just generalise. Some think that the universe *is* far too complicated to have happened by chance and assign its existence to 'nature' leaving the whole question unanswered until perhaps one day they find out for themselves: By then it could be well nigh impossible to gain the attention of those left behind so that they can report back: Also the opportunity to live a more happy; hopeful and purposeful life may have been missed.

No longer can we be satisfied with a child-like belief, we need tangible evidence. If life after death and talking to the dead is bunkum there seems little point in all the pain and suffering if one day we are snuffed out like a candle in the wind. We may use our imagination, we may entertain ideas that appear to be contrary to common sense, and sometimes it's hard to separate fact from fantasy, but let us not give up our reason or our sanity, let us take a look at the evidence with an open mind. Even though these questions are primarily about evidence people still insist on seeing them as religious which is mostly a system of belief. Sceptics can have a sense of intense anger at being faced with someone who they believe is quite plainly 'unbalanced' and who is trying to convert them to something. Of course this subject does shed light on the existence of the religions and I have to use the parlance of the day; words like 'God' and 'Heaven 'and Angels: These are labels which are sweeping generalisations, simplifications, caricatures almost but highly inspiring whilst for many not imagined as a real people living in a real place. I want to use logic and enquiry to try to understand the origins of our life on earth and beyond, all of which I find deeply fascinating. In terms of science there is no contradiction with the facts that have been discovered it is simply a consideration of an alternative explanation for the origin of those scientific laws which are the foundation of everything we know: It all sounds so improbable but here we are living in wonderland. In the world of psychic phenomena we have to come to terms with some admittedly very rare events but also quite common everyday experiences which perhaps have been misinterpreted. There are oddities in life that don't quite add up including the experiences of countless numbers of individuals which suggest the existence of other realities. Extra-sensitive people can pick up atmospheres; moods and feelings about events that are due to happen, that some disaster is about to occur or even as trivial as knowing that the phone is about to ring. Whilst these moments don't seem to be registered by everyone it would appear that all human beings have a largely unconscious awareness of the immediate future and what other people might be feeling. Body language aside where do these signals come from? As yet they are not detectable but in any case how can we know what hasn't happened yet? Many of the bereaved claim to have seen or sensed the presence of the dead and are likely to be told it's merely the habit of a lifetime but there are those who look for verifiable evidence. For that it is to those sometimes seemingly odd people with odd beliefs that we must turn for they have spent a lifetime struggling with a view of existence so different to what mainstream science tells us: Some become more public and spend their lives trying to connect ordinary people with the spirit world. For too long mediums have been seen as figures of fun with an advert featuring a toffee crisp wrapper floating down onto the séance table or the shrill cry of *"Is there anybody there?"* from a very eccentric Madame Arcati played by Margaret Rutherford in 'Blithe Spirit.' This subject is in fact something very serious and based in the real world which has a very positive effect on many of those who consult mediums. It can however have a very negative outcome if wrong assumptions are made or if mediums are relied upon to make important choices then putting life on hold or anxiously waiting for a prediction that takes twenty years to come true or not at all. Heightened sensitivity is an ability which runs in families consequently there are some for whom it's a burden: Like a monarch some feel as though they are sentenced to a lifetime's work like it or not. Others enjoy the peace of mind; the reassurance and the comfort it can bring to others. In my experience the future is very commonly told through mediums but proof of survival which is stunning, less so, though there is plenty of everyday rather trivial but very evidential information and more than enough to prove the case many times over.

You may wonder if all of this is worthy of serious consideration however the main focus of many researchers has been to disprove this phenomena and believe you me whatever doubt you may have about the following most of these men and women also had the same scepticism including some who were extremely antagonistic: Even mediums need proof that what they are getting is true. In 1848 Hydesville, New York, the Fox sisters were the first to use knocks as a code to communicate with the 'dead': What began with childish games was the beginning of a craze in America which spread to Britain in 1852. Within the British 'Society of Psychical Research' whose membership read more like a copy of 'Whose Who' there was a determination to prove that the whole thing was a fraud which was rife over here and easy money at that time. But fraud often copies the genuine and after a considerable amount of investigation into some quite outstanding physical mediums, together with other areas of serious research in the general population, the conclusion was that survival was the only answer that fitted the facts. Those early researchers included highly accomplished men and women who are still household names some of whom are listed at the back of this book. This is a subject about which most of us have inbuilt attitudes primarily it is seen as farfetched; impossible; the province of the simple minded and totally not provable. It can be blamed on imagination; mental illness; fraud; staged magic; a lack of proper scrutiny; the almost God-like properties of the brain and bad press. There are catch phrases like 'No one has ever been back' 'Mediums are frauds using cold reading' 'Conning people for money' Whilst there have been cases and probably still are I think it's often that some people are just not very good at mediumship: That is linking with spirit telepathically and accurately passing on what they have received. It is with a heavy heart that I read about investigations into this subject that allegedly failed. Because life after death is not seen as feasible and everyone who believes it is deluded a favourite experiment is to set up a fake séance or medium to show how gullible we all are. It is however a fact that most of us try to make the messages fit our expectations. The vast majority of mediums are ordinary sensible people from policemen to housewives who confine their psychic observations to friends and acquaintances. Some work within Spiritualist Churches and turn up at meetings in all kinds of weather only asking for the bus fare and a cup of tea. The more spectacular phenomena tends to be held in private which causes a lot of suspicion however a lot of effort is taken to make it foolproof. No one has explained to me why sensible thinking people would spend years fooling themselves when in fact it is often the scientists who they mistrust because they seem to prejudge and be antagonistic from the outset in a situation which is sensitive to mood. Nowadays members of the magic circle perform tricks which have become increasingly mind blowing, well beyond the capability of any random medium who generally comes from a very ordinary background and often was very young when the particular phenomenon began to manifest for instance: When a child at a funeral asks "Mummy how can Uncle Bert be dead when he is standing next to me?" he/she is smacked or told to keep quiet. In the meantime I have quoted strange, fantastic but deeply thought-provoking material that has come from mediums and their *'inspirers,'* the so-called dead. Finally when it comes to the question, 'Why is there anything at all why isn't there just nothingness we are truly left with scenarios that we cannot even imagine. And so I hope you will come with me on a journey that is stranger than fiction. I have enjoyed exploring the unknown and feel sure that you can share that enjoyment with me. Spirits and spirit worlds, miracles and magic remind us of our childhood days or perhaps of 'primitive' people whom we assume think like children, they don't know that that which they experience is scientifically impossible. I suggest that in future years it is we who will be looked upon as primitive and narrow-minded, clinging to our belief that if we voyage too far we will fall off the edge of the world. One day the clock will stop for you, as it will for me and we might find ourselves desperately trying to tell our nearest and dearest that we are still very much alive; we may however find that this is almost impossible. When we hear people talk about us we might wish we had known when we still had the chance to put things right and like millions of others, we will have to stand by and watch as our loved ones keep on keeping on, and try to help in whatever way is possible. So many of the bereaved feel that they have unfinished business even if it's only that they didn't get the chance to say goodbye or how much they loved the one they have lost. The issue of survival leads to all sorts of questions such as, 'Why is the natural world so violent?' 'Why are little children allowed to suffer?' and 'Is someone over there looking out for me?' The human mind is legendry in its ability to create, to imagine, to fabricate and the work of mediums has always been thought of as being trivial, humorous and even fraudulent. - In truth sensitivity can be a life-long burden but what they do is extremely profound. They give us hope and an insight into our life on earth and they open the windows of heaven that we might peep through.

THE FRAGMENTED SELF.

If the material world has no more substance than a rainbow, the individual, the person, you and me, are just as intangible. Fundamental to our experience of life is our own personality and that of others, it is sacred and it is what we are. If we were all of us identical, like machines, we could love everyone or no one; there would be no competition, no point in living. There would be no individuality, no colour in life, yet that precious thing which is me, which is you, is composed of a series of fragments; a collection of memories and emotions; details in the genes; almost automatic reactions to experiences usually beyond our control. Brain damage, due to accidents and strokes, has shown which parts of the brain affect not only the physical control of our bodies but also how we feel about, and interact with, the world about us; for instance in our *beliefs and attitudes*.

When the connections between the two sides of the brain are severed the subject seems to act like two people inside one head, each in some measure unaware of the other. Normally the two halves can communicate, even when separated but, by covering one eye, one side of the brain can be shown an object that the subject cannot describe because speech is controlled by the other side of the brain. Apparently we identify with the left side of the brain; the right side seems to have its own identity.

When shown a *'photograph of a naked girl'* 'subjects gave *'amused grins'* but couldn't say what they really found so funny.' (P38. 'Manipulation.' Erwin Laush. Fontana. 1972)

Colin Wilson wrote about patients whose hands wanted to do opposite things. The first man was trying to stop his hand unzipping his trousers, a second man was holding his other hand to try to prevent it from hitting his wife and the third man had to sit on his hand because it was interfering with his jigsaw puzzle. (P18. 'Afterlife.' Colin Wilson. Harrap. 1985)

A change of personality or perception is perhaps easier to come to terms with when it is due to brain damage but there are some mental conditions that are not as yet understood. There can even be more remarkable divisions in the mind as in multiple-personality syndrome and regressive hypnosis both of which have a lot in common with the phenomenon of an alleged spirit speaking through a medium in trance. (Sometimes called channelling.) Whilst I imagine it is possible for an individual to unconsciously build a model of another personality in the mind, almost like play-acting, it is obviously more evidential if the 'communicator' is someone you know.

We inherit our habits, our state of health, and at least some parts of our character, from our ancestors and as individuals we are the result of a series of chances or accidents. Our personality can change with the weather, with circumstances, with experience and most drastically with health. When the brain is damaged and the person we know changed out of all recognition can anything survive these tragic events or are we just left with a memory of a wonderful and loved individual? Have we seen the last of him or her, has that old familiar face become a grotesque distortion of its former self, is the one we loved like a crystal ornament that has been shattered into a thousand pieces never to be put back together, or a machine that has gone wrong and is unrepairable? Even the moment of death is not so clear-cut; life is still present in the cells of the body; cells which some believe have their own rudimentary consciousness. - Similar pond-dwelling organisms that have no brain or nervous systems are still able to make simple decisions.

After a bump on the head Manchester schoolgirl Vicky Wilmore wrote back to front for a whole year until another bump restored her to normal. One man was unable to read but he could write perfectly well and a woman could not see in 3D - everything looked flat like the page of a book: There are individuals who wake one morning to discover that they have acquired a foreign accent. When some think of a number they see a shape whilst days of the week might be certain colours, these effects may be viewed as if watching a screen inside the head that is superimposed upon ordinary sight. Sights; sounds; feelings and colours can be intertwined so that when they listen to music, for example, the experience can be truly all-embracing and wonderful in a way which is denied to the ordinary listener. This phenomenon is called Synaesthesia which I understand is some kind of leakage between different sections of the brain. These are understandable malfunctions of the brain but as we know certain conditions, not only drugs, can alter our perception of events. Patients with brain damage help researchers to understand how different parts of the brain deal with the various aspects of our sight and even our understanding; it is the latter that I find most fascinating.

When one man looks around him he sees only a jumble of coloured shapes and another is unable recognize objects. He draws a brush and refers to the bristles as legs. A third man can't remember faces and only knows his wife if she is where he expects her to be. A fourth cannot recognize moving objects. Researchers have found that the visual process refers as much to memory as it does to what it is seeing. ('Brain Story.' Prof. Susan Greenfield. BBC2. 1st August 2,000.)

Perhaps that is why optical illusions work, why we can see faces in the fire and mediums can read from a jumble of shapes in tea leaves etc

Peggy Palmer ignores the left side of her visual field both in the real world and in her imagination. She draws flowers that have the left half missing even though she can still see the whole scene.
At the age of eight Graham Young sustained brain damage when he was hit on the back of his head by a car. He is blind to the right of his focal point with both eyes but he can still guess correctly when there is movement because a second link from the eyes to a higher part of the brain is

still intact and this is known as blind vision. I presume that this is the mechanism by which we drive the car between the gateposts without hitting them.

Prof. Ramachandran believes that one half of the brain tends to deny unpleasant realities whilst the other challenges that denial that is unless it is damaged. In which case the patient can believe the most ridiculous explanations as a substitute for the truth for example one lady believed that her arm belonged to her husband.

The Professor also suggests that religious belief or feeling might be a product of a faulty brain. He also says that *'someone has calculated that the number of possible permutations and combinations of brain activity exceeds the number of elementary particles in the Universe.'*

('Phantoms in the Brain.' Prof. V.S.Ramachandran. Channel 4' Television. June 2,000.)

Noah Wall was diagnosed with spina bifida and hydrocephalus whilst in the womb. He was born on the eleventh of the eleventh of the eleventh at eleven-o-clock with only two percent of a normal brain. He is now eight and his brain is eighty percent normal. He can do a whole list of things doctors said would be impossible and is now learning to walk. He is such an adult happy-go-lucky child who it *seems* has defied logic.

In people who have half of their brains removed during childhood, the remaining hemisphere rewires itself to allow the person to function as if the brain were intact.

<u>(The Independent)</u>

It also seems that there are new ways of trying to re-programme the brain. Those who used the robotic strap-on legs found that they had re-learned to walk once the equipment was removed. This makes me wonder if some re-wiring of the brain takes place when points of view and attitudes are changed for the better or for worse. It's really incredible how something simple like a water infection can make people talk utter nonsense and it makes me marvel that most human beings are relatively sane. Certain brain seizures can transform the patient into little more than a mechanical man robbed of the ability to make decisions or of any kind of emotion. - Could this mean that the real me is merely a function of the brain? Scientists are trying to work out what coordinates all of the various sections of this lump of grey matter. What is it that experiences that virtual reality world within the cranium, is it like staring at a TV screen and when the picture develops a fault we are unable to switch it off or to turn our attention in another direction? When confronted with a child genius it might be tempting to believe that he or she has lived before but when we see some of the very badly mentally handicapped for instance in a coma it's just as hard to believe that there could be a highly evolved person gazing at us through those windows on the everyday world and yet computers have shown us that in some cases there is. If the individual has no way of communicating we can't know whether or not the conscious self is trapped inside. In 2010 it was discovered that a man who had been in a coma for four years was fully aware of his surroundings. Once given the means to communicate some have revealed a high degree of intelligence but it's as if completeness depends upon being able to store memories, experiences and arguments in a structured way. Perhaps sometimes they must remain at a simple level because brain damage means that they can't organise anything more complicated.

In terms of seeing is believing a hallucination is assumed to be created by the brain or the imagination however it may on occasion be triggered from something outside the cranium as in hypnosis, or more commonly mediumship which brings with it the opportunity to assess the possibility of minds in another reality.

REALITY AND ILLUSION

'Life in the abstract is already a riddle, reality turns it into a riddle within a riddle.' (Vincent Van Gogh.)

The big question is whether mind is independent of the body or simply a by-product of nature. In all this scientific pulling apart of a human being, however we describe it, there is that certain something, which is beyond the ability of science to weigh and measure. There is an essence, a lasting quality which like love itself plays on the emotions, rules the senses and directs our innermost thoughts. There seems to be a part of us that goes on unchanged and which observes; this is the real you which experiences the changes of fortune, of personality through all the ups and downs from birth, through our youth and onto old age. To survive death there must be a soul, some *thing* that is indestructible. According to scientists there is a certain part of the power of reasoning that seems to be going on at the same time as the brain is going through its calculations or through the sequence of events before we decide what to say or what to do. Either the brain can do two things at once in a way not yet understood or there is an extra component, an operator, a driver, or a separate mind that uses the brain like a computer. Lori and Reba Schappell are two American ladies that are joined at the head sharing a part of the same brain yet they have entirely normal but different personalities: They do however share certain senses and feelings.

Just like the spaceman with his radio and TV links we have all of the apparatus to communicate with each other, not hand made with wires, transistors and microchips but an infinitely superior system that has grown just like any plant grows. These electrical signals sent to the brain are all we know of the world, we are like a man who is confined to his own little room and sees only the images presented to him on his television set. He cannot imagine the cool summer breeze or the refreshing spring rain on his face, he knows nothing of the joy of flying or of seeing around him that panorama, that vista, that view as far as the eye can see, he is only aware of the image that is presented to him on a small screen inside his head, his own virtual reality. Without his senses he wouldn't know about the mighty universe or be able to wonder what it all means, he doesn't even know if it really exists outside his own little world. By the same token we don't know if everyone has the same view of reality.

I have met individuals who are sensitive to underlying energies; emotions and intuitions beyond clever guess work and whilst these feelings seem to be at odds with our mechanical universe they appear to be passed on through the genes. These abilities often manifest themselves in being able to reach outside of our everyday senses into other realms. We might think that all of these strange facts about human beings explain a lot about how some people see and hear things which others can't and that there is no point in looking for fanciful explanations however it is the bizarre unreality of our human situation that I am trying to illustrate and it is the evidence of the existence, or influence, of separate independent minds with which we are ultimately concerned in survival. One can be quite sceptical when an individual appears to speak like an entirely different person with completely different memories until someone we know comes through. This phenomenon is incredibly interesting but where non-evidential material, i.e a medium giving philosophy we have to trust the individuals's track record. After listening to many, many mediums sometimes delivering messages that are hard to decipher its incredible how it is possible to read between the lines and how other sensitive's pick up on the fact that the message is sometimes being given to the wrong person: That the message sender doesn't clear this up is an indication of how difficult the process can be. Whilst a medium is psychic a psychic who doesn't practice mediumship can do an awful lot without any connection to the spirit world they can certainly read character, history and future from an individual's energy field.

We are of course no nearer understanding consciousness or its relationship to the material world. Our so-called logic tells us that our body is nothing more than a machine that one day will be consigned to the scrap yard, its useful days over and its presence soon forgotten in the busy workaday world but our intuition is trying to tell us that there is more to it than that: That the machine had an operator and that the human body is an object brought to life by something which is separate and which endures. Remember also, nothing in the present mechanical way of looking at things can explain telepathy, intuition, psychic phenomena, precognition, near-death and out-of-the body experiences and things that go bump in the night.

ARTIFICIAL INTELLIGENCE

If the human being is only a mechanical man and nothing more it should be possible to build a computer which is alive. A computer however has no more intelligence than a ordinary flashlight and generally operates upon information fed into it. However if it could be programmed with the right responses so that it displayed all of the reasoning power of a human being, how would we know the difference? Eventually computers might be grown like plants and after a long period of evolution self-learning computers will have surpassed the ability of countless numbers of genius' and will have the ability to 'think' outside the box, on the move as an android, a life-like robot. Whilst we have always thought of computers as clinical and unfeeling some scientists believe that one day they will be able to give them emotions and they might even use food as a power source! The memory could be saved long after the rest of it was consigned to the scrap heap and even be put into a new computer to live again. If that machine was powered by a nuclear battery and capable of physically adapting to changing environments surviving even the destruction of earth, for example, by escaping into space, its memory span could last forever and it could become a God in its own right: But would it have self awareness, would it be alive, would it be a living freak, would some passing spirit try it on for size? I doubt it as it would seem that the energy to move objects in our dimension originates from a human being or a particular hot spot generated by a past powerful event and much used by 'ghosts.' It would appear that the energy that gives the human body life is an energy activated by the mind and instigated through the will of our being. Perhaps one day brains will be grown in a laboratory and installed in robots; a gruesome thought reminiscent of Frankenstein's monster or Doctor Who's Cyber men: Already they are trying to combine the much faster brain cells with micro chips. The question is can a brain think without a spirit to give it life?

Neurons in lockdown: When brain cells (Taken from the brains of mice) are trapped in microscopic cages, they grow long appendages to __make connections with each other__*. ...The team's next step is to investigate if the cells can transmit electrical signals to each other.*

(Stanford University. New Scientist May 2020)

In Australia lab-grown human brain cells have been taught to play ping pong. It is not known if they have any awareness. (The 'Conversation Newsletter' Jonathan Este. Nov 2022)

According to Professor Kevin Warwick, a Cyberneticist at Reading University:

'If machines can be made as intelligent as humans ... (they) will take over and either destroy us or force us to lead 'a slave-type existence.' 'People who say it will never happen are not being realistic.'

(P12. 'The Observer Magazine.' 17th Oct. 1993.)

I notice that Steven Hawking has also sounded a warning note on this subject suggesting that it could be the end of the human race. (2015)

If the world became a place where androids ruled it would be like a huge machine making pointless decisions leading to pointless actions with no thought, feeling or awareness and beware any humans that fell play to its mindless impulses.

MEMORY

Consider the invention of memory, an amazing system that records every second in the lifetime of a human being. Fundamental to our individuality as human beings is our memory of those we love, of who we are and of our experiences. One day we might be able to have access to the memories of the dim and distant past, or even of other people, in order to learn, to understand or even help fix their psychological problems. The evidence suggests that such a system already exists in nature. Some mediums like to hold a personal item such as a watch or a ring to link with both spirit and the sitter which seems to make contact much easier. When Psychics hold an object they can read its history and link with the person who last handled it; the process is called Psychometry. I once recorded a reading during a flower service where each bloom was identified with only a raffle ticket. Whilst I was able to recognise meaningful points and was very impressed generalised readings can often apply to anyone. Psychics can be very specific finding minerals deep underground by dousing a map of the area. This can apparently be quite a lucrative occupation but what use could nature possibly have in 'evolving' such a system? - The same might be said of the enormous capacity of the human memory.

One man called Shirichefski consciously remembered everything and couldn't concentrate because he was constantly *'rummaging'* around amongst a jumble of images. ('BBC Radio 4.' 9th August 2001.)

Whilst Bob loved being able to remember the whole of his life, Jill's disturbing memories never went away. Aurilean also liked having his memories. - Brain scans at Hull University indicated more visual activity whilst he was remembering; Jill too remembered in pictures.
(The Boy Who Could Remember everything. Ch, 4 Sept 2012.)

Lyall Watson described an experiment in which the subjects had to recall the contents of a room filled with *'a vast collection of unrelated objects.'* Under hypnosis all the differences between each individual were *'almost completely ironed out.'* Everyone could remember almost everything. One subject mentioned a newspaper in a frame and when asked for more information began to *'recite ... masses of detail from columns of fine newsprint that it is humanly impossible to resolve from a distance of twelve feet.'* Dr Watson states that *'Even a vulture with its special telescopic acuity, probably couldn't manage it.'*

(P287. 'Lifetide.' Lyall Watson. Coronet Books. 1979.)

Kim Peek, on whom the 1988 film 'Rainman' was based, is a mega savant. He *'has memorized more than 9,000 books, can predict the weather, and has been called a latter day Mozart.'* He can, *'memorize telephone directories at lightning speed.'* And both eyes can read a different page at once. *'He is an expert in at least 15 subjects'*

('Sunday Telegraph' Magazine. 23rd Jan. 2005.)

Twins Flo & Kay Lehman are savants who can remember what happened on any particular date including, music, musicians, the weather etc. They can even tell you what day a particular date was before they were born. They don't know how they know but when they do they describe themselves as being *"Joyful – Peppy."*

(Extraordinary people Channel 5 Television. 2008.)

When a neighbour's son asked Paul McKenna for help with his biology exam Paul knew that everything was supposed to be stored in the mind. So he told the young man that he would be able to remember everything he needed to pass his exam which he did. It was the only 'A' and in the rest of his exams he only managed to get 'Ds' and 'Es'. Paul was able to uncross his fingers because what he didn't tell him was that in the absence of the required information the mind would just simply make it up.   (BBC Radio Two)

Neurosurgeon Dr Wilder Penfield was amazed that the brain could remember such a vast amount of information, much of which was not accessible to the individual.

Though he could trigger the recall of even very trivial memories by touching various areas of the brain with an electrical probe, he never discovered how those memories were stored. The subject remained very much aware in the here and now whilst these events were recalled. Because of this Penfield concluded that the brain and mind acted like a computer and programmer.

('Closer to The Light.' Melvin Morse MD with Paul Perry. Bantam Books. 1991.)

An individual who has been brain damaged, affecting his short term memory, is still a complete human being in terms of his awareness of himself, his likes, dislikes, personality and his personal history, but he is stuck in a time warp. Every time he asks about close relatives and is reminded that they have died he is stricken with grief all over again. If our lifetime memory is retained within our being and can be accessed via the unconscious mind there seems to be no inkling of that in the following.

Patsy lost over 30 years of memories. She didn't know how to put the plug in the sink, or wash up, or cook; it was like living someone else's life. Her daughter said she was different in many ways but she still had her outgoing personality. ('U.K. Living. '10.3.97.)

When Sarah recovered consciousness after a brain operation she noticed that her husband looked considerably older and wore strange clothes and she wondered who the young girl was by his side. When she eventually went home that too looked different and there were other houses on the once-vacant plots of land. The furniture wasn't the same as she remembered and there were new-fangled gadgets like the microwave and the dishwasher. Instead of three young children there were four teenagers and even the car looked like something out of the space age. Sarah herself dressed and acted like a twenty-three-years old, playing loud pop music around the house; sixteen years had been irretrievably erased from her memory.

('The Unexplained. 'Presented by Robert Stack. Sky One. 3.9.94.)

What I find interesting is that a slice of time has been taken out of the memory rather than simply impairing it. When some people come near to death they experience a complete and immensely detailed and life-like review of their life in seconds. If there is another part of us which is indestructible which perhaps registers far more detail than we were consciously aware of at the time Patsy and Sarah's reviews will be complete.

We now turn our attention to the phenomena some of which is more familiar but contrary to everything science has to offer.

HYPNOSIS, A WORLD OF ILLUSION.

If we can question our physical perception of the universe can we rely on our mental view of it, is there another way in which we can arrange the matches, a way we haven't thought of? We have all changed our mind at sometime or other but what about when that mind change is taken out of our personal control? Nowadays we are used to the idea that the personality that we hold so sacred can be modified by hypnosis. The nervous can become confident, likes and dislikes can be changed but to see something that isn't there or not to see someone who is, is literally changing our view of the world. Paul McKenna tells his subject that he is about to meet an ugly woman the idea being to laugh at his reactions as he is asked to take her on a date. When he meets this young lady face to face he sees not what the audience sees, someone who is very attractive, he sees a wrinkled distortion of a very pretty face with teeth which are all blackened and broken. Alternatively the subject may see, and talk to, someone who isn't there at all like another man who kisses a broom in the belief that it is his favourite singer. Sometimes I get the impression that he or she is aware that some kind of play-acting is going on, I suppose rather like in a dream but with others what is experienced is entirely realistic and convincing. These clever party tricks have profound implications for our own personal reality and like all facets of hypnosis are interwoven with the whole concept of the next world where the mind appears to be able to create its own environment.

Ruth was actually able to create an apparition, a double of her psychiatrist which only she could see, feel touch and smell and which acted and spoke like a normal human being. (P2182. 'The Unexplained.' Orbis.)

When the hypnotized brain is told that an (imaginary) hand has been placed over the eyes it does not register light.
The ability to judge between reality and imagination is blurred when experiencing hallucinations through illness,

drugs or even extreme tiredness. The subject may see inanimate objects come to life and dance around the room. One TV programme showed the insertion of teeth implants into the bone, with the assistance of the hypnotist the pain was described by the subject as two out of ten.

The implications are that mind is not simply a by-product of matter but that it is superior to physical things. We are used to this idea in the unreal world of dreams and fantasies but in the real world, mind can do things that would seem to be impossible. We each of us have super-human capabilities that are rarely used and do not appear to be under the direct control of the conscious mind. Physical scars have appeared when subjects under hypnosis were 'reliving a past life' and 'experiencing' being flogged or knifed: Then there is the question of the stigmata, the scars of the crucifixion have appeared on the hands and feet of over 300 people since Francis of Assisi; for example, there have been many intriguing stories written about Padre Pio, an Italian monk who exhibited bleeding stigmata from 1918 until his death in 1968.

Frederick Myers cites a case recorded by Dr Biggs of Lima in which a subject was hypnotized and told that every Friday a red cross would appear on her chest.
('Human Personality and its Survival after Bodily Death' by Fredrick Myers "Longmans." 1907.)   (From the Journal of the, SPR., vol. Iii, P100.)

Lyall Watson recalled a well-known case in 1950 of a 16 year old boy with fish-skin disease in which a boy's body and hands were covered in warts and a shell-like substance as hard as finger nails. Each time he was hypnotized different parts his skin returned to perfect normality but some three years later, in an effort to remove the remaining warts he wasn't able to be hypnotized at all. A further eight sufferers couldn't be cured by hypnosis. - Colin Wilson suggests that after the first sessions the Doctor had discovered that the disease was caused by malformation of the actual cells of the skin and was therefore incurable. – In other words as long as the Doctor believed that hypnosis would work, it did so. (P64. Beyond The Occult Guild Publishing. 1988.)

In two independent trials a number of women increased the size of their bust and decreased their waist measurements after being put into a light trance.

(P177. 'Trance.' Brian Inglis. Paladin. 1989.)

The skin of a hypnotized subject may be touched by a hot implement without burning, the slight blisters healing more quickly than would normally be expected. Conversely a cold object will cause blistering if the hypnotist suggests it and, when told that an imaginary hand is gripping the arm, finger marks appear on the skin. An arm can even be held in the air for long periods of time without fatigue and under self-hypnosis the body may exist without a normal supply of air as in the burial of eastern holy men who return as large as life without suffering any sort of brain damage. The Indian rope trick is apparently an exercise in mass hypnosis which only works on those standing nearby. When hypnotized the human being can detect faint smells and sounds normally only sensed by animals; other feats like jumping fantastic heights and lifting heavy weights are sometimes performed by ordinary individuals during moments of crisis.

Whilst running away from a machine gun a soldier said that he had *'360 degree vision.'* Another man reported seeing bullets *'almost like baseballs so visible that he could dodge them.'* (P129. 'The Light Beyond.' R.A. Moody. Pan Books. 1989.)

The placebo effect is well known, one woman was given sugar pills as pain killers knowing that there was no active ingredient but the pain returned when the trial stopped. And so what! Perhaps we simply don't understand how much control the mind really has over the body. We have yet to face the fact that it can have a physical effect far beyond the boundaries of the cranium.

There are times when an individual's personal perception of reality is altered, not by a hypnotist, but by something else and in my research there are plenty of cases where people have seen what no one else can see or who can't see what others can see, as if something or someone, has edited, the TV picture within their minds: Sometimes this happens only once in a lifetime when they are in desperate need. It would appear that there is some other, unseen and unnoticed, controlling intelligence, or intelligence's in the world of man which can when required, influence his actions, his thinking and even alter his personal view of reality without him being aware of it. It would seem that help may be given; either in time of crisis or where life-changing decisions are being made; and even in more mundane daily circumstances; directly through that individual or by influencing a third party.

Some investigators who don't believe in hypnosis and telepathy never-the-less in effect use them to explain away what witnesses *think* they have seen. Hypnosis has however proved to be able to open the door to the subconscious and in turn to other states of being. Various depths of hypnosis have been employed to reach beyond the body with all kinds of exciting results. One of these is the *apparent* emergence of a different personality whether it is from a *past life* or a *guide* speaking through a medium.

WHO AM I?

The problem of different personalities in one head has a direct bearing both on our individuality, the possibility of the dead speaking through a medium or intruding into the mind of those we call insane? To see a medium entranced by another *'personality'* makes one wonder if this some kind of unconscious play acting.

At an Estelle Roberts' séance *'Bessie Manning'* gave her name and address and asked that her mother be brought to a later meeting because she was so unhappy. The sitters had so much confidence that the proceedings were genuine they immediately sent a telegram to Mrs. Manning who was able to attend a later séance and confirm details given by *'Bessie.'* (Maurice Barbanell. 'Psychic News.' October 1977.)

Even those who are not host to an external mind can display remarkable changes in personality. An experiment conducted by Prof. Lie'geois shows that subjects in trance are really in two, or even three, minds. It would appear that there is always a part of us observing and analysing, even when we are totally unconscious and remember nothing of what has happened.

'"M.Lie'beault entranced Camille, and at my request, suggested to her that she would neither see nor hear me any longer. ... (When) other persons present pricked her she quickly withdrew her arm; If I pricked her she felt nothing. ... (I spoke to her) as though I were an inward voice of the subject's own. ... I said, ' Camille is thirsty; she will go to the kitchen and ask for a glass of water, which she will place on this table,' She seemed to have heard nothing and yet after a few moments she executed the prescribed action, with the quick impetuous movements often observed in the somnambulic state ... asked why she brought the glass ... she (said) she had not moved; there was no glass on the table. When M.Lie'beault addressed me she was astonished and thought that he was talking to

the wall. ... I said, 'Camille will take from the pocket of from M Lie'qeois' the bottle which contains eau de Cologne ... and smell the delicious scent.' 'She ... came straight to me, found in my pocket a bottle of ammonia, uncorked it and smelt the odour with delight. (P384.)

In other experiments conducted by *Prof. Janet, Le'onie*, a slow melancholy woman, was found to have two other personalities: one they called *Leontine* the second *Le'onore*. According to *Le'onore, Leontine* was noisy and frivolous whilst *Le'onore* herself seemed to be a more sober character liable to pass into a state of ecstasy. (396.) *Leontine*, sometimes frightened by the interruption of *Le'onore's* voice which is giving her advice, describes herself as being dazzled by a light on the left side. When *Le'onie'* was in her waking state the trance personality *Le'ontine* began to remove her apron as previously suggested by *Professor Janet*. He then called *Le'onie's* attention to the loosed apron. *"Why my apron is coming off!" she exclaimed.' 'Next day Professor Richet hypnotised Le'onie again.' Le'ontine* commented. *"I did what you told me yesterday! How stupid the other one looked. ... why did you tell her that her apron was falling off? I was obliged to begin the job over again."* Le'ontine became a personality in her own right with her own chain of memories and was even able to write letters which she hid to prevent *Le'onie* destroying them.

(P376. 'Society of Psychical Research. Proceedings.' F.W.H Myers. 1888-9.)

'Felida X was dull and taciturn; but on recovering from a headache she was transformed into somebody who was jolly, vivacious and intelligent: She knew about her life as the dull Felida but the dull Felida knew nothing of the life of the bright one who took over for a while and married her lover. Later the dull one started coming back. She was gloomy, disliked her husband and was often ill, though never seriously, whereas the bright one was healthy. The dull one would remember nothing of arrangements made

by the bright one who gradually took over.'
('Trance.' Brian Inglis. Paladin. 1990.

Hypnotisme double conscience. 1887. Prof E Azam.)

A medium that is prepared to allow another personality to take over may use deep breathing and concentration to induce a detached trance-like condition. They might begin to feel colder and make involuntary movements then completely give way to another persona whilst hearing every word that is spoken through them and listening impassively as if at a distance. Some feel as though they are half out of their body, others claim that they are watching themselves from the other side of the room whilst another person is speaking through them. A few are entranced without even being aware of the fact until they regain consciousness but they may have had experiences 'elsewhere.' As with dual personalities one *'spirit'* does not necessarily share the same knowledge and memories as another or even with a medium in trance. I can't imagine how such divisions can appear in the brain, just as puzzling were those who had lost their memory over a defined time frame. When a spirit returns to earth he/she is returning to old thought patterns; controlling a human being at first can revive vivid memories of an unpleasant death whilst memories of life in spirit may become more distant.

Both Mrs Vlasek and Vincent Turvey allege that they have spoken through a medium whilst out of the body.
(P93. 'Man Outside Himself.' Prevost Battersby. Psychic Book Club. 1943.)

'W.T.Stead' says that, *'At first this taking possession of a strange body is an extraordinary experience for him. To feel that he is really himself in another's body; to see with eyes that have not precisely the same kind of sight that his had; to hear with ears that receive sounds differently from what his own did; to think with a brain to which he is not accustomed - this is at first grotesque.'*

(P15. 'Communication with the Next World.' 'W.T.Stead' through Madame Hyver.

Automatic writing. 1914.Greater World. Almorris Press Ltd.)

Expressing one's self through someone whose mind is still active is fraught with difficulties. Maurice Barbanell Psychic News editor and medium for *'Silver Birch'* recalled the guide of *'one of our greatest mediums'* who made a *'certain pronouncement'* then said, *'"That is not my view. It is an idea that is dominant in my medium's subconscious mind. The only way that I can continue to function in freedom is to express this dominant thought and get it out of the way."'* (P80. 'This is Spiritualism.' Spiritualist Press. 1959.)

'Feda', the control of Mrs Osborn Leonard, certainly seems to have proved her individuality to The Reverend Drayton Thomas. He writes,

'My 'Father,' my 'sister' and 'Feda' habitually refer to each other in a conversational way, just as anyone might speak of friends and fellow workers. They allude to each other's characteristics, to their skill or limitation in communicating, and speak of knowing each other intimately in their life away from earth. One can hardly convey the impression received by these multiplied touches of reality.' He then relates incidents which demonstrate that *'Feda'* had been present in other locations including a direct voice séance where voices were heard not through the medium's lips but from another part of the room.
(P161. 'Life Beyond Death with Evidence.' 1927.
Drayton Thomas. Psychic Book Club 1928.)

At a Leslie Flint Séance his cockney guide *'Mickey'* was recognised by a new sitter who used to buy papers from him every night. After his disappearance the man made enquiries about him and was told that he had been run over by a bus. This confirmed what *'Mickey'* had previously said. (P124. 'Mediums and Their Work.' Linda Williamson. Hale. 1990)

Spiritual healer George Chapman becomes a different personality in trance; *'William Lang'* was once an ophthalmic surgeon at Moorfields eye hospital. Doctors, family and patients who knew him have been able to converse with him on both medical and personal matters about which George, an ex-fireman, could never have known. Lang's very sceptical, daughter Lyndon went to see Chapman and came face to face with her father and later gave George the brass plaque from her father's place of work. ('Psychic News.')

J. Bernard Hutton, Diplomat; writer; journalist; visited Chapman because he had failing eyesight. After two healing sessions with *'Dr Lang'* Hutton wrote,

"An incredible story? Well incredible or not the wonderful improvement of my lamentable eyesight is a fact."

(P190 Out of this world J. Bernard Hutton. Psychic Press Ltd. London.)

As far as I can see this case provides us with all of the proof we could ever need about the validity of mediumship at its best. Using hypnosis to retrieve *memories of former lives* muddies the waters even more when trying to separate fact from fantasy. Recently I watched a documentary on the subject of multiple personalities: Four young women with alter egos ranging in number from about twelve into the hundreds. These are of all ages from different countries but speak very lucidly and have totally different stories and personalities. Sometimes the host is blacked out and unaware for periods of time. A Perfectly normal *young 'man'* will take over when the girl is under stress. He was asked if he got along with the others he said he was told he had to, to progress. (((A term often used by Spirit communicators.))) Others allegedly in the background were clamouring for different things in an ice cream shop but they all seemed to be there only to help and be helped. These struck me as genuine individuals but I wish they had been asked where they were at other times.

(My Multiple Personalities and me.. A Crackit 5 production for 5 star .August 2018.)

The possession theory does *'appear to account for the different levels of intelligence, varying (perceived) physical attributes, and differing genders, as well as the multiplicity of skills, talents, desires, ages, styles of handwriting, tastes, voices, vocabularies, allergies, and illnesses expressed by different alters.'*

(Multiple Personality Disorder: an alternative theory' Laura Harrison 2006.)

ALIENS.

The possibility of physical life existing in other dimensions will come into the story several times. Some ancient civilizations tell of visitors who came from the stars, *if* this is true are these star men still around or will they return? In only a few short years mankind has made tremendous advances, the NASA SETI program spent millions scanning the skies in a massive search for intelligent signals. If there is life somewhere across the vastness of space, there is a possibility that it may be thousands of years in advance of ours both in knowledge and technology, what could they possibly have come up with in all that time? These God-like beings would surely be able to affect any repair to the human body that could mean that they would be incredibly old and very overcrowded too. They would probably have developed the ability to traverse the universe, and perhaps through other dimensions, which means beyond our senses! Some claim to have seen E.T's walk through solid objects, both they and their craft appear and disappear like ghosts and if this were true they would certainly be aware of our existence, whilst we are obviously unaware of theirs. One or two mediums do make this claim and that might explain why, if they are out there, they have remained undetected. As the process of hallucination and clairvoyance can be indistinguishable from each other this may explain why some spaceships and alien beings seem to appear according to the fashion of the day in terms of the look and design of the space ship and the appearance of the alien figure. A fine theory for an individual but when groups of people see the same thing, and very close too, I find it hard to dismiss therefore to me it remains an interesting possibility.

It seems that our own spirit has lived lives on all sorts of worlds before coming to earth in which case we might have a stronger connection with them than we could ever imagine and that might include some very interesting relatives. According to *'Veronica'* evolved beings from other spaces are among the human race to support and guide. (Issue 149) Some experts think that we would be wise to keep as quiet as possible in view of the suffering which the 'uncivilized' populations of earth have undergone at the hands of the 'civilized.' But if space really is teeming with life, why aren't we fighting each other? Perhaps spiritual advancement has gone hand in hand with increased technical knowledge. In that case the extra terrestrials, whether from another dimension or another galaxy, might decide that we need to evolve in our own way. During the Second World War many pilots saw lights and ghostly aircraft, that they nicknamed 'foo fighters' - Each side thought that they were their opponent's secret weapons however I believe that were human spirits i.e. our own kith and kin. In more recent years one fighter pilot told how he flew alongside a UFO for some five minutes but rather than feeling threatened he had a feeling of peace. It was only when his weapons system locked onto it that it pulled away.

(John Dunn Show. BBC Radio 2.)

Rosalind A. McKnight during an OBE describes being taken to a space ship which like Doctor Who's Tardis, is not bound by time. It is manned by beings that are highly intelligent that have a '*high love energy*' and can pick up '*thought waves*' from '*past*' present or '*future.*' Negative energies from earth have an effect on '*all levels of the universe*' ...The challenge for them is to try '*to raise the consciousness of the earth.*' (P104)

There are also beings on a higher rate of vibration than earth '*who make contact* '...but '*who don't have the same concern for our welfare*' The higher beings will not intervene unless there is a danger of self destruction which would '*set up reverberating patterns of destructive energies throughout the galaxies.*' (P107.)

('Cosmic Journeys.' P106 Rosalind A. McKnight. Hampton Roads 1999.)

Maybe NASA is engaged in a game of 'blind man's bluff', stumbling blindfold around the universe whilst at the same time being surrounded by unseen watching eyes both living and 'dead'.

COINCIDENCE

Whilst it would be odd if coincidences never happened the following stories do not appear to fit in with our normal view of reality. Could it be that in some strange mathematical way all things in time and space are linked or is it evidence of the interconnectedness of man's unconscious intelligence? Bearing in mind the mathematical certainty that coincidences do occur I sometimes think that, as in dreams, the subconscious somehow influences our everyday, waking life. Most of us experience weird coincidences, although less complicated than the following, and many claim a noticeable increase in such incidents after turning their attention to so called *'spiritual matters.'* - Perhaps they are simply noticing a phenomenon they haven't registered before?

'In 1967 Essex policeman Peter Moscardi mistakenly gave the new number of his police station to a friend as 40166 instead of 40116'... Late one night he and a colleague noticed a factory with the door open and the light on. There was no one there but...*'the telephone rang,'* and *'it was (Moscardi's) friend'*...ringing 40166 the number he had mistakenly given him. This was the one and only time...*'that the factory manager had forgotten to lock up.'*
(P2230.112. 'The Unexplained.' Bob Rickard. Orbis.)

There was a man living in Derby who was listening to Frankie Lane's rendering of "The cry of the wild goose," when a Canadian goose crashed through his window; a driver who was thrown from his car and killed whilst his car ended up against a tombstone bearing his name and American writer Anne Parrish who, on her first visit to Europe, found the book she had as a child whilst browsing through bookstalls in Paris. - It was complete with her maiden name on the flyleaf. (BBC Radio.)

The following three cases are from the Richard & Judy TV show 'This Morning.'

One lady backed into a car in England then later in America, she reversed into another car and was amazed to find that it was driven by the same person. The two became firm friends. ('This Morning.' Richard & Judy. ITV 18.6.94.)

When London taxi driver, James Bell, received the accounts from his accountant he discovered that they actually belonged to another James Bell who owned a taxi, 690 DLO. James number one's taxi was 609 DLO. Both wives were Elizabeth's, called Betty. Both eldest daughters were named Sheryl, and both youngest daughters were called Gillian. The two taxi drivers used the same bank and of course the same accountant.

Susan from Manchester rang in to say that an important letter, addressed to her had been blowing around in the wind for some two hours and then wrapped itself around her leg as she walked down the street two miles from her home. ('This Morning.' Richard & Judy. ITV. 7.11.97.)

That story suggests a little more than pure coincidence.

We also have the strange idea that some events seem to happen in threes. It might well have something to do with the law of averages but when you hear of two funerals you can't stop yourself from wondering who might be next. Add to all of the forgoing the possibility of seeing events that haven't yet happened and the ordinary workaday world becomes decidedly extra-ordinary. There is strong evidence that all is not as it appears to be, evidence which simply will not go away.

TELEPATHY

Telepathy is the idea that one mind can send messages to another mind; Whilst at the moment its working is not understood and not even acknowledged by many scientists it is sometimes used by sceptics to explain away mediumship though Carl Jung wrote, *'so called telepathic phenomena are undeniable facts.'*

('Psychology and the Occult.' P135. Ark Paperbacks London 1982.)

I imagine that telepathy occurs more often between two people that have some empathy or as I would say as a Television Engineer, between individuals who are in tune with each other just as the television aerial needs to be in tune with the transmitting aerial. Telepathy at a distance appears to be one of the simplest ways to demonstrate an effect which cuts across present scientific understanding: It would seem to be quite easy to repeat with the right subjects. In his book 'Psychical Research' Sir William Barrett F.R.S. describes simple experiments that demonstrate the 'transmission' between two people (both in the 'Normal' and 'Hypnotic' State) of all kinds of information. This includes tastes; sensations; images and facts including finding hidden objects and carrying out simple pre-determined tasks. Initial experiments involved using children in various games: The person transmitting the thought might touch the person who was to receive it, lightly on the shoulder or forehead and concentrate upon the image, word, or instruction that he wanted to send. The person receiving would then say what was in his or her mind at the time. Effects such as tasting vinegar can be passed through several intermediaries all touching in a chain. A subject under hypnosis cannot register a bitter taste given directly but will attempt to spit it out when the hypnotiser tastes it. (P72) At first it was thought that the information was somehow passed by involuntary physical means until eventually it was realised that it still operated at a distance. Sometimes the process didn't work and over the months the subjects lost their ability to receive perhaps through *'weariness or anxiety for success.'* (P61)

('Psychical Research' Sir William Barrett Williams & Norgate 1911)

There is a lesser known condition caused by extra receptors in the brain and known as *"mirror-touch synaesthesia"* in which the subject can feel emotions, physical sensations and even the pain of others.

(Dr Miriam Stoppard. Daily Mirror 28.12.2018)

Whether this is purely a condition of the brain recalling sensations when the subject sees someone touched or showing an emotion (In effect mimicking) I can't say but following are examples of pain and emotion felt at a distance where there was no conscious knowledge of what was sent. It brings to mind a husband's pains during a wife's pregnancy and pains shared by twins perhaps during some trauma. Mediums also commonly feel symptoms of an illness including pain from people sitting opposite.

In the Soviet Union, Yuri Kamensky *'imagined that he was strangling his friend'* Karl Nikolaev who simultaneously *'began to feel suffocation.'* *'Nikolaev's 'EEG patterns showed such drastic changes that physicians, who were present, wanted to stop the test out of concern for* (his) *health and even his life. When Kamensky imagined beating Nikolaev and 'transmitted' this thought to him, Nikolaev sensed severe pain and almost fell out of his chair. This telepathy spanned five hundred miles from Moscow to Leningrad.'* Nikolaev had no *'ordinary means'* of knowing what Kamensky would choose to send. In previous tests no *'emotions'* or *'feelings'* were sent, the experiments being confined to *'visual images.'* (P232)

('The Mind Race.' Russell Targ and Keith Harary. New English Lib. 1984)

In tests by Psychologist Marilyn Schlitz at California, subjects were measured with lie detector-like sensors that showed that the_unconscious knew the exact moments they were being watched via a TV camera.

('Out Of This World.' BBC1. Tues 31st July. 1996.)

A polygraph machine, wired up to one twin relaxing in a separate part of the building, showed a violent <u>unconscious</u> reaction at the instant of a loud unexpected bang which shocked her sister relaxing on stage.

('The Paranormal World of Paul McKenna.' Man alive. Carlton 24.6.1997.)

Now we are in the age of MRI scans, where there is a moment of strong empathy between two individuals a certain part of the brain becomes active in both people. The difference between the person sensing real pain, and the person imagining the pain, can also be seen.

(Psychic World. July 2004. Michael Colmer.)

Consultant Neuropsychiatrist Dr Peter Fenwick connected couples up to EEG machines. With those who were close, sounds played to one were shown to be picked up by the other in a separate room. These tests are easier to asses than the flow of information between medium and spirit communicator because we know what information is being sent and received.

Talking to you through the medium of the mind is exceptionally difficult because the mind is a force to be reckoned with. It has an innate determination to explain; follow a line of reasoning; one thing follows another and so when I say something which is conjuring up in your mind a certain thing the brain naturally wants to fulfill its obligation, its purpose and fill in the gaps When we come to you we are often very lucky that you can switch off and let us speak unhindered however there are plenty of times when you allow your mind to listen to and assess what is coming through which allows it to interfere. (2019.)

In the spirit world all communication is by telepathy therefore language is no barrier so I guess that you must remember not to express words in the mind if you want to keep them private.

PRECOGNITION.

The man is in his early sixties and in reasonable health; he has never had a day's illness in his life; quite suddenly he makes a momentous decision to tidy out the garage. Later in the week he sorts all of his papers out and on the weekend visits his sister whom he hasn't seen for twenty years, a week later he is dead: Told to me by his widow but not an uncommon story. Perhaps his unconscious mind has told him that his body is about to stop working but what about *'Ron's'* case. Days before he was killed in his lorry *'Shirley'* was playing an old record, one that they had heard hundreds of times. When it got to the part that obviously triggered some unconscious feeling of his impending death, he flared up and told her to turn it off.

Seven years old Leanne always played outside but on this particular day stayed indoors close to Mum who told me she was shocked when she suddenly told her, "I want to live to be a hundred," The next day Leanne died of smoke inhalation in a fire at her home. Life after death might seem to some to be impossible and to be able to see events that have not yet happened, even more so, yet many, many people unquestioningly accept the premonition!

Psychic Artist Coral Polge recalled a portrait of a young boy she drew for a Mrs Margaret Hansford, with it she received impressions of a railway line and an accident. Fifteen years later Mrs Hansford happened to meet Mrs Joan Saville from Australia and showed her some of Coral's drawings. *'Suddenly she spotted the portrait of the young boy and said without hesitation, "But that's my brother!"'* She *'could hardly believe her eyes'* when she read the notes on the back. Her brother loved trains and was killed *'on the crossing'* whilst she was looking after him; she was only a *'little girl'* herself.

(P166. 'Living Images.' Coral Polge. Aquarian Press. 1985.)

There certainly seems to be an element of planning with foresight in that story. - Even the little we understand about time makes fascinating reading. Because of the many years it takes for TV signals to travel the vast distances in space, someone out there could be receiving our old, early black and white television programs like the 'Flowerpot Men' and might even be trying to understand their strange language. Light waves that left the earth in 1066 might just now be reaching some distant planet. To them our present is still in the future because they cannot yet see it. For this to happen in reverse, which is for our future to be seen before we have even lived it, reality would have to be very different from our present view of life. The Dutch clairvoyant, Gerard Croiset, took part in many experiments at Utrecht University in which he was successfully able to describe the occupant of a certain seat in an audience, days before the event, even though each place was taken at random. In some cases the subject had no intention of attending but had changed his or her mind at the last minute and decided to come after all.

Dr Dean Radin of the University of Nevada showed psychics 140 scenes on computer. 100 were peaceful and 40 were shocking. Tests showed that the body was anticipating the shocking scenes before the computer had chosen them. ('The Paranormal World of Paul McKenna.' 24.7.97.)

According *to Prof. Brian Josephson, a Nobel prize-winning physicist from Cambridge University, 'So far the evidence seems compelling, What seems to be happening is that information is coming back from the future. 'In fact it's not clear in physics why you <u>can't</u> see the future. In physics you certainly cannot completely rule out this effect.' ...' Virtually all the great scientific formulae which explain how the world works allow information to flow backwards and forwards through time'* (Dr Danny Penman. 'Daily Mail.' May 2007.)

'Myers' again:- '... we would be bold and adventure into the imagination of God ... we turn again the pages of the Book of Life and read the future of our race. We gaze upon a drama that has not yet been enacted upon the earth, the

vague echo of which is sometimes caught by prophets and soothsayers. We perceive the wanderings of those begotten by us, the fate of those who are of our blood, who bear upon their foreheads the seal of kinship with us. And indeed many of us sorrowfully close the book of life when we have gazed into a future that is not yet for men, sprung out of the Unknown, out of the boundless sea, which I must again remind you, is the creation of the all-pervading imagination of God.'

'... the power to enter the third subjective state and thus to follow the future as well as the past, page by page, is bestowed only upon those souls whom human beings-to use a trite adjective-would call "advanced" or would hail as "spiritually developed."'

P127/8. 'The Road to Immortality.' '*F.W.H.Myers*' through Geraldine Cummins
(Trance Writing.) Psychic Press. 1932.)

If the future can be foreseen it brings in the question of time travel. Physicist Kip Thorne suggested that we might be able to go through a *'worm hole'* in hyperspace and arrive two or three years ago.   ('John Dunn Show.' BBC Radio Two, 12.8.94.)

In other words someone might just appear and announce that this theory had been put into practice and he or she was the first to test it out. His friend and colleague Stephen Hawking believed that time travel can't possibly be true because we would be inundated with sightseers from the future but apparently he has now changed his mind though perhaps only in terms of seconds. One objection was that a time traveller who murdered his grandmother when she was young could not have existed but it occurs to me that he wouldn't then exist in the first place. Physicist Paul Davies suggested that if you tried to change the past for instance by shooting someone, the gun would jam. In 2005 scientists calculated that it would be impossible to change the past and as we shall see when we try to change events for our own advantage by seeing the future whilst out of the body, fate does seem to step in at the crucial moment. An answer to Stephen Hawking's objection might lie with the time machine itself. Time travel might only possible from the time that the machine was switched on but would be able to receive messages from the future. I am sure that if it ever happens legislation will be brought in, in order to control what influence people in the future would be allowed to have over our present time: Certainly all bets would be off! Physical time travel however might prove to be impossible though it seems that when we move outside of the physical dimension we can actually view the past, present and future but are unable to influence or change events. - Perhaps after all we do have visitors from the future watching us both seen and unseen! In the film *'Back to the Future,'* Marty sees Doc Emmett the inventor of the DeLorean time machine gunned down which would leave him stuck in the past but the Doc is not dead because he has read the warning note left for him in 1955 and is wearing a bullet-proof vest. 'Doctor Who' uses this trick now and again going back to a time just before the disaster in order to alter the course of events.

If the block universe theory is correct past and future are still in existence. (Horizon. July 2018) *The events in the block are there for all time: they do not change. So, as a time traveller, it's not as though I suddenly appear at a past time. It's always been the case that I am located at that past time. Nothing a time traveller does changes anything in the block. Instead, what the traveller does at any time makes that time, and later times, the way they are. That means that we know that some things we attempt to do in the past, fail. We know that Hitler rose to power in the 1930s, so we know that if our time travelling future selves try to prevent this from happening, they fail. But that doesn't show that our time travelling selves don't succeed in doing lots of things in the past. For all we know, the reason the past is the way it is, is in part due to the presence of time travellers.*
(ABC Science. Associate Professor Kristie Miller is the joint director for the Centre for Time at the University of Sydney. Posted 2018.)

A lady told me about two members of her family, man and wife who were sitting on the settee, suddenly both saw flames, helicopters and boats. A couple of days later the wife's brother was one of 167 killed in the Piper Alpha oil rig disaster on the 6th of July 1988.

Michael Bentine also had upsetting experiences with foreknowledge when during the war he began to see the faces of certain members of bomber crews as skulls, they proved to be the ones who didn't come back. (P140) At a later date the face of his son Gus changed into that of a corpse and he knew that if he flew with his friend Andy the two would be killed. The prophecy tragically came true. Bentine always quoted a saying by Goethe 'The future casts a shadow behind it '

(Michael Bentine 'The Door Marked Summer.' Granada. 1981.)

Eddie Slasher had a vivid dream in which he spent a full day at school: then was killed by speeding white Mercedes. Next day everything happened as he had dreamed it. He knew the exam results in advance and the joke his friend told him but he waited until the White Mercedes had passed safely by before crossing the road.

(P108. 'Explorations Out of the Body.' Kroshka Books 1997.)

There are studies which prove a change in the pattern of routines prior to a disaster as if some individuals followed their instincts and for example avoided a plane or train crash. There are also plenty of incidents of warning voices saving the day. But the first thing everyone wants to do when confronted with the idea of foreseeing the future is to make money and whilst it is not uncommon to see future events through dreams I believe those who make money out of them would be quite rare. We had examples of least three people who perhaps wouldn't have won had they not dreamed of winning, including John Godley, later to become Lord Kilbracken, who had had a series of dreams in which he would read the results of the days races, before they had been run: These were verified by a national newspaper. But Eddie Slasher's out of body excursions didn't work so he tried a new tactic. He made several attempts to see the lottery numbers (posted next day at a local garage,) during OOBEs but it seems that fate always stepped in and spoiled his plans. Remembering the numbers on his return to his body was his greatest obstacle once his view was obstructed the next time he forgot one number. Out of two choices (one was correct) he picked the wrong one. Eventually he concluded that the future is just a probability however (*the more significant or otherwise life changing the event you witness in an OOBE the more probable it is that (it) will come true.*)

(P119 'Explorations out of the body'. Kroshka. Books 1997.)

In tests at the Stanford Research Institute psychics were able to locate a site, which a random computer had chosen from a number contained in sealed envelope. This ability to foretell the future was put to good use; an organisation called Delphi was formed by Russell Targ, Keith Harari, and business consultant Tony White, to earn money with which they could fund their research. They made nine correct predictions on the commodities market, some against the trend, simply by deciding whether silver would go up or down 25c on the following Monday. They made profits of over 100 thousand dollars. ('Horizon.' BBC.TV. 1983.)

Chris Robinson was undergoing a series of tests at the University in which he would dream about specific locations that he was to visit. (He would score ten out of ten.) On Saturday the eight of September 2001 he was in the hotel bar with Prof Gary Schwartz and numerous witnesses and told them of a nightmare involving planes crashing into tall buildings and thousands of people dying. This was not a part of the experiment and was forgotten by Prof Schwartz but Chris continued to have more dreams. When 9.11 happened Prof Schwartz was "*traumatized*" not only by the event itself but also by the thought that he might have done something to prevent it.

('The Man Who Dreamed the Future.' Channel 5. 10th September 2007.)

One of the real conundrums of prevision is in respect to reincarnation. It is said by some *"communicators"* that the life not yet lived can be viewed before birth and even altered to fit in with the things the individual wants to learn. Does that mean that Hitler chose his life or did he alter it by making bad choices? Allegedly some choose difficult lives both as a challenge but also one might say, 'Someone has to do it.' Prof Ian Stephenson has researched this scrupulously for many years. Some cases seem to indicate the return of family members which in some cases might have died prematurely, this is tricky as the youngster might have picked up information due to its closeness with the family: There are cases of youngsters who have recognised people they have never met and other subjects who. seem to have had a previous life with complete strangers. There is always the thought that someone is picking up impressions from a person in spirit but in many cases there are physical birth marks such as bullet wounds which have indicated how they have died: I will return to this subject a little later.

To think that we are all trams on a fixed route rather than busses with a certain amount of free will would seem rather pointless; a life without a reason to hope. One individual under hypnosis was able to see his own future and asked the hypnotist to remove all knowledge of it before being woken otherwise he might try to avoid something that had to be experienced for his progress. Trying to tell the future as in replying to a question is fraught with difficulties. Perhaps the future shows different possibilities only one of which actually occurs also anything that comes through the human mind is unreliable.

When the future is told it can be misleading it diffuses the possibility, the hope, the expectation and when that future arrives it is never anything like the picture that was painted in the mind of the one who received that telling. (Feb 2021)

There is a different phenomenon a feeling of knowing; a certainty which is beyond logic as when I *knew* I was going to win the raffle at work. Certainly female intuition can be pretty accurate in the form of feelings; though I think predictions tend to come quite randomly and without warning. In my experience thoughts from spirit can be different from imagination in their unusualness perhaps more so in my case as they were attempting to prove themselves. Some mediums' guides refer to life here as being 'In the linear.' If time doesn't exist that really puts us in deep water. We can only know that a prediction was right with hindsight. There have been predictions of an accident which turned out to be a near miss. Someone we know just missed being crushed; his wife being very sensitive was immensely worried in the days before the incident. I remember a story told on Richard & Judy's show someone got a strong impression not to put the Child's car seat in the usual place which was the back seat. A lorry did come careering down the hill it was a near miss but it could have completely demolished the rear of the car. One man came seeking advice from mediums at Norton Spiritualist church: He had premonitions all of which were horribly upsetting; like the birthday cake candles still lit but the little boy wasn't there. It came tragically true as he was so excited that he ran out of the house and was killed by a passing car. It's as if our friends in spirit have to standby as we walk under a bus. The two messages that I am aware off were only understood by the congregation with hindsight: I remember one lady was hit by a truck after leaving the meeting. It makes me think of a soap where the writers have to allow an exit for some characters or indeed a change in the plot. I remember being told that they were not allowed to tell us anything that hadn't happened yet. Having said all that I must say many times over the years I have been shown a road in my mind's eye. Once during a very harrowing time I saw a well-lit bridge with rails of support leading to an island where the grass was a brilliant green: Suddenly my work circumstances changed for the better and I was moved to a different location near home. Sometimes the road can be bumpy and not very bright, lots of trees might obscure the way ahead but I must emphasise that these views were not specifically looked for, which would give the brain an opportunity to fabricate: They were incoming as are random thoughts which might indicate imminent obstacles. No jokes please.

Consciousness is something we take for granted and yet there are moments when some people experience another consciousness which they say is indistinguishable from our day-to-day waking state. Some people claim to have stepped into a past or future scene that to them was tangible and real, not simply imaginary places but ones which had existed in the past or would exist in years to come; ghosts of the future. - Like Sir Victor Goddard who flew over a deserted airfield, in 1935, and saw mechanics in blue overalls working on yellow planes, one of which was a monoplane of a type unknown to him. Four years later the airfield was re-opened. By then the colour of the overalls had been changed from brown to blue, and the planes, now monoplanes used for training, were painted yellow instead of silver. (P80. 'The Paranormal.' Brian Inglis. Paladin 1985.)

We will leave the last word to Albert Einstein who said that, *people like us who believe in physics, know that 'the distinction between present and future is only a stubbornly persistent illusion.'*

BEYOND THE SENSES.

Playing around with interesting ideas is all very well but does it really tell us anything about the facts? Not long ago man discovered new worlds beyond the horizon; could there be other horizons mankind has yet to go beyond? There must be an infinite number of things we don't know and of which we have never even dreamed. At the moment they are talking about solar systems existing in places previously thought out of bounds and until relatively recently, galaxies were only a theory, but modern telescopes have revealed millions of them.

The universe revealed to our senses is "but one of countless universes that move together in time, that lie against one another, endlessly, like the leaves of a book. And all of them are as nothing in the endless multitudes of systems that surround them."

(H.G. Wells. 'Men like Gods'. Cassell and Company, Ltd. 1923)

In view of all the superstition and misguided belief of the past we look at the physicists with disbelief. Their talk of a multiverse seems to be as much of a dream as heaven itself. Is it so impossible to believe that life just might exist in another part of the spectrum outside of our narrow field of physical senses? According to the Chief Astronomer there could be another universe just millimetres away and we wouldn't be aware of it. If that universe was filled with intelligent life it would be like those countries separated by the mighty seas which grew and evolved alongside each other on the same planet completely unaware of each other's existence but how easy to laugh and say that's completely different. It wasn't that long ago that there were still people who believed in a flat earth, how wrong they were.

When the microscope was first invented everyone was shocked to discover a world of living beings that existed in a glass of water. It's not unreasonable to imagine that there are beings somewhere in the vastness of space, how do we know that life does not exist beyond the senses, outside of the narrow range of frequencies that the human brain is aware of? Just because someone is blind doesn't mean that there is nothing to see; the deaf are still surrounded by sound and to all intents and purposes when the people down the road are indoors they are beyond the reach of our senses. There are infra-red and ultra-violet light waves, which are above and below human sight; sound that is beyond human hearing and radio waves with different television, radio and communication channels occupying the same space. Is it possible that matter too radiates out in exactly the same way, a universe within a universe? This could mean that solid landscapes exist in exactly the same place as where you are now and if mind and body are separate then perhaps mind can have adventures in other dimensions physical and spiritual. If you can retune your consciousness you might find yourself in beautiful countryside, or a city, or a concert hall, or any one of countless places that make up the spiritual worlds. Thus it is said that in the spirit world; like messages that exist side by side on the same broadband cable when you are out of tune with one another you are also out of sight. Some people are born with the ability to travel to these other realities but for some it's a once in a life time event through accidents or a near death experience.

Everything is energy and that's all there is to it. Match the frequency of the reality you want and you cannot help but get that reality. This is not philosophy this is Physics.

Albert Einstein

We have been so conditioned to the idea that heaven and spirits are for the simple minded, vestiges of primitive beliefs, and yet the evidence suggests that what has been thought of as a dream world, a fairy tale, a figment of man's imagination, is in fact as real as the Australian continent which lay undiscovered, (By those in the West!) until courage and ingenuity found the way and that, like many of the early Australians who were forced to leave their families in Britain never to return, the so-called dead are looking out on some new horizon.

Some might think that by all the laws of common sense this must surely be impossible. Common sense however is limited by our lack of understanding of the facts; facts which in the following story are the laws of physics, some of which, no doubt, have not yet been discovered. The truth about a greater reality has yet to be revealed but we all *think* we know. I laughed when I read a particular scene about a group of house painters and decorators in 'The Ragged Trousered Philanthropists.'

Rushton thought that it was ridiculous that *'Hawstralia is on the other side of the globe underneath our feet. ... If it was true wot's to prevent the people droppin orf?'* Sweater agreed. *'If it was true we would be able to walk on the ceiling of this room ... but of course we know that's impossible.'* Grinder added that if the earth were round all the water would run off except for a little bit at the top. Rushton observed that as for the globe whizzing round in space at *'twenty miles a minit'* If a skylark hovered for a quarter of an hour *'when the bird came down it would find itself 'undreds of miles away from the place when it went up.'* And *'if a man started out from Calais to fly to Dover, by the time he got to England he'd find 'imself in North America, or pr'aps farther off still.'*

(P353. 'The Ragged Trousered Philanthropists.' Robert Tressell. 1914. Granada. 1965.)

If life truly is an illusion, death no more important than changing your socks; grief as pointless as crying because your nearest and dearest has popped out to the shops for a few minutes; if the human race were to think of themselves like actors on a studio set with others waiting in the wings to come and go as the plot dictated; if we could leave the body every time the going got too hard; then how could we experience the strong emotions which life generates and what would be the point of it all? Without these emotions we would be like computers; unfeeling, uncaring not fearing loss because loss would be impossible; not seeking success because there would be nothing to gain; absolute boredom for an absolute eternity. In a perfect world the whole story of mankind with all of its drama and colour, would not have been written. If the illusion is to be maintained that we are totally separate from each other and that this old earth rolls around all day on its own, that we are to be self reliant, self sufficient, then it is essential that that illusion is so foolproof that the human mind cannot see behind it, see it for what it truly is; a learning environment created to generate strong emotions where choices have to be made. The prospect of living in one spot for the whole of eternity, heavenly though it might be, is unthinkable.

Existence, it would seem, has been purposely divided up into an infinite number of places and at any one time our view has limits imposed upon it just like the simple example of the horizon. Life has been scaled down to a manageable size; the illusion of the desert island is complete; we must learn by surviving; we are on our own so that we can make our own decisions according to our own experience. If this illusion, which is truly a matter of life and death, has been made so perfectly then how do we break through to the truth that lies behind it all? How can we disprove the illusion, how can we prove that there is anything there at all? The written word can make the open minded think but the skeptics would need evidence brought to them, perhaps only a medium can do that. If there are worlds beyond the atom we are faced with a different problem from that of distance in miles, it is the distance between one dimension and another. How can instruments made with the stuff of our dimension reach out into a world of a different making? Until that breakthrough is made we have to build our knowledge upon something that shifts like sand - the human mind. Unlike the Wizard of Oz we cannot see how a creator might pull the levers of the material worlds; all we know is that there are scientific laws by which everything operates. Were these laws created by higher intelligences, the product of countless minds working in concert? These minds would not be confined by time or the limits of the human brain with its finite memory: They would contain the wisdom of eternity. Physics is one area of research which manages to come up with some pretty way out ideas the other is Psychical research in which Physicists were amongst the first drivers of investigation into the possibility of survival. The accepted wisdom in science treats the brain like a God without asking how feasible it is. It may for example seem reasonable that out-of-body and near-death experiences are a kind of hallucination or the product of a vivid imagination or even drugs but it doesn't explain how individuals can see events, sometimes at a distance and in the case of the near-death experience at a time when the brain is completely shut down and eyes closed. The admittedly hard to believe research is automatically dismissed because so many scientists or individuals *believe* that it is impossible. In an existence where there is no death or suffering one could sit on a cloud playing a harp for all eternity and there would be; no adventure; no challenges; nothing to learn; no real individuality! In our reality free will must be paramount. Here we can be a unique person and live a life with all of its experiences good and bad, you learn what it is like to be you. Far from St Peter directing us to the left or the right we judge our own life to determine where we went wrong. We need food to keep our bodies alive; we can kill or be killed;

we can give up our life for a friend and so on. We can be a parent and can also experience bereavement and thus appreciate other souls. We have to make choices; make an effort; we can discover, invent and so on. We can return to earth that we might have challenges and adventures and we can start again with all of the wonder and magic of a child unencumbered by past mistakes.

The world is structured in such a way that mankind must learn to live alone; on his wits; in his own time; in his own way. And in doing this must learn to interact with other souls who have other ideas; other priorities; other likes and dislikes: To list all of the patterns that this world has created would take an eternity. It is the richness of the earth environment which is so useful so helpful to souls learning and experiencing and undergoing various trials and tests that they might see things in a different light that they might understand their fellow souls their comrades in arms their enemies even. None of these things are possible in spirit where harmony is the order of the day (But what about the planes where there is no harmony?) *In breaking the harmony of the spirit world much has been learned both by those who are undergoing the process of being human and those who are shadowing them; guiding; helping; to keep the whole show on the road. From all points of view the earth has been a great success despite the wars; despite the pain and suffering and despite all the mistakes and ill thinking we have come through unscathed and unharmed. The lessons we have learned have made us stronger; more able to cope and more able to help. To succeed in life we must have a strong presence of mind trying all the time to solve problems; to find solutions; to use our ingenuity; to know how to respond. All of the different strengths and frailties are teachers to compare one state of mind against another; to be in the moment and yet to be absent; to go with the flow of events or to direct them; to change course; to use force; persuasion; anger; regret; and so on. And all these things are part of the wonderful mix of emotions;*

strengths; weaknesses; and attitudes which is the world of man. (2019)

The open door which is the spirit world had to be sealed that humans could not readily access the source of their being that they would have to stick at it, follow the plan, be devoid of any knowledge that they might make their own way, investigate, imagine, follow all kinds of trains of thought to get to where the truth resided; to imagine something greater than themselves which would help them in their downfall their piteous existence, their troubles but would also guide the way to more thoughtful realms.(Feb.2020)

Just about everybody that you've ever met is here. They all want to be remembered for what they did; for who they were; for old times; good bad or indifferent they have a certain fondness, the good old life; the happiness; the hard work; the determination to get on. Their lives were not always easy; sometimes tragic; off times gruelling, but the magic that a life can bring to a spirit being is beyond all measure like a wonderful picture painted by a great artist each life is unique. Each story is a story to be told to inspire to bring happiness and richness in its wake. The little we know of one another causes us to be critical, imperfect in each other's eyes and when we reach the spirit world we are enlightened, we are able to truly understand the blemishes and the beauty of each soul; the bonds; the links; the caring and the sharing. (Oct 2019.)

There are all kinds of scenarios in life ... and we have seen them all over the centuries passing through each phase; each fashion; each war; each peace; from starvation to plenty; from king to beggar and from beggar back to king again. A thoughtful and enriching experience that is not available in the spirit world as such... there are things to come which will delight man's heart, make everything all right and shine a light on the life that he has lived be it in darkness or in light all come to the same end via different routes. (November 2020)

RELATIVITY

Time is fundamental to our whole experience of living but Einstein has shown that our time might be different from someone living elsewhere. Some physicists are saying that time might run backwards in some parts of the Universe which could mean broken things coming back together and people growing younger!! We might also imagine that our dim and distant future could be somebody else's present: Someone, somewhere across time and space, could have been born, lived a full life and died of old age whilst we were getting out of bed. Perhaps we have eaten breakfast, gone to work and returned for our evening meal whilst he or she has merely crossed the street. How could we possibly relate to such beings, perhaps just as with the living and the 'dead' the only thing we would have in common are our minds.

Our time is regulated by the speed of our bodily movements; in other words, how fast we can actually put our thoughts into action, and how many things we can do before the earth turns a complete circle but in an accident everything can appear to be in slow motion. When we dream, time may stand still and during a short nap we may have a terrible nightmare, or a wonderful experience, which goes on for ages. Our experience of time varies according to our interest or lack of it and in the next world it is said that this is literally true. There is a suggestion that time is an illusion and that there is only now. If that were true then perhaps memory had to be invented not only as a necessary function of a physical body but as part of an artificial way of dividing existence into small packages.

Perhaps it's just a question of scale: Each atom is the centre of an enormous force but that force might only be enormous in terms of a human being: To the powers that be, the mighty universe may be like sand blowing in the wind: The whole universe might easily fit into a teacup. Perhaps we are like ladybirds on a leaf, completely unaware of the gardener or of the greater world outside and all that it means to an intelligence of an infinitely higher order. The intricate workings of a watch are impressive, but a human being that was only an inch high would see it as a large piece of clanking machinery. Beings from other planets could be as tiny as a flea or as tall as a mountain and to them we might be as small as a mouse or as big as a dinosaur and yet people who claim to have seen ET's describe figures that roughly conform to the human scale and design perhaps because they have evolved using a variety of the same principles that permeate the Universe. To sum it up in the words of Douglas Adams,

'Due to a terrible miscalculation of scale the entire alien battle fleet was accidentally swallowed by a small dog'
(Hitchhikers Guide to the Galaxy)

The idea of the variation of scale within the boundaries of our own universe is something that we can well imagine however, the universe itself may only be large with respect to the human body. The difference between our world and the unseen is something else: There is a force which is active in both and that is a power which is invisible; cannot be quantified. It does not seem to have the observable qualities of the energies in our world except for its association with the brain which in itself is fallible and in no way eternal. It would appear that this fundamental force is mind; mind which controls the body however it cannot of itself in our physical reality move mountains or even the tiniest object with the exception of a handful of very rare people: A subject which in itself could fill another book.

DREAMS

Mystics say that life is really a dream:- One lady recalled an experience when she was about fourteen. - She awoke, dressed, had breakfast and went to school then as the bell rang she was startled to find that it had all been a dream and that she was still in bed. She began her day again but this time someone at school threw a book that hit her. Once more she awoke in bed and by now she was so disturbed that when she arrived at school she told a friend about her experiences and suggested she pinch her to see if she was really awake. Her friend did so and once more she woke up in bed. Eventually, when later on in the day nothing untoward had happened, she concluded that she was finally awake. These experiences gave her a sense of unreality never quite knowing if she was dreaming or not.

('Everyman.' BBC1. TV. 12.11.85.)

If out-of-the-body experiences are real and there truly is a world of spirits, if sometimes we leave the slumbering body on the bed, then surely we would expect to have at least some glimpse of that other world filter through the dozing, dreaming brain. Rarely do we try to react against the preposterous things we see and do in dreams, we are often just a passive observer but there are always dreams that stand out because of their clarity. It could be that we see things that we couldn't possibly have known about unless some part of our consciousness had been there at the time. Prophetic dreams can be made to fit the facts afterwards, especially with generalised events such as air crashes and it is always better if they have been written down at the time or told to a third party. We may dream of someone we haven't seen for years then meet her the next day or we might see a loved one we have lost and feel the immense relief that he is not dead after all, only to awake and find him gone. Once in a while the reality of the dream subdues our grief and the sceptic would say that the mind is playing tricks but something inside is telling us that it was real. Some people say that they never dream however when the brain is sound asleep it will have no memory of any out-of-body adventures thus some researchers have recorded everything they could remember in the first waking trance-like moments.

In the past the Prophets often received their messages through dreams or through the interpretation of other people's dreams in which symbols were bringing the message. Like Joseph (The Bible. Genesis 37) who dreamed that he and his brothers were binding sheaves in the field. His sheaf stood upright and his brother's sheaves bowed down to him. Who could have guessed that he would one day become a great power in the land where his brothers would not recognise him and would bow before him? In another story King Nebuchadnezzar had a dream which he wanted his wise men to interpret without actually telling them anything about it. Only Daniel could find the answer, - through a dream. Pure legend you might think, dreams are dreams. Psychologist David Ryback thought so until faced with a group of people who happened to be talking about dreams that had come true. Unable to find a satisfactory explanation he decided that this would form the basis of his next research project. He was stunned to discover that out of 433 students one third reported having at least one psychic dream. He felt however that only eight per cent *'could not be explained by ordinary happenings.'* David's colleague Leticia Sweitzer wanted to find out more and began to ask friends and relatives and the people she came across at shops and parties. Two out of three had had psychic dreams. One in three could remember at least one impressive story many of which were sometimes quite accurate previews of events that would not occur for days or weeks after the dream. There was the bank robbery that happened the very next day and another highly detailed dream involving a car crash in a red Volkswagen and a blonde with a baby. Three months later the dreamer and her husband moved opposite to such a girl and the accident happened exactly as the lady had dreamed it. In the emergency room later her husband said,

"You dreamed this and I didn't pay attention to it."
There were unusual deaths and even a death that hadn't
happened: - It was an obituary that had been given publicity
but which turned out to be the wrong person.
('Dreams That Come True.'David Ryback, Ph.D. & Letitia Sweitzer.
Diamond Books. 1988.)

The first person I mentioned this book to told me that her
son had dreamed of a man in black and then another man in
black reading a book. Some weeks later he was astounded
when he recognised the man in black after entering a
church. This was priest number one. The second man in
black was reading from the bible at his brother's funeral.
After a woman dreamed of winning the jackpot on the one-
armed bandit at Las Vegas, she and her husband drove
through the night and at the second attempt she won.
Another woman dreamed that her deceased brother asked
her to place some numbers in a jar and he would then help
her to draw out the winning lottery numbers. - And she did!
In February 2015 in the early hours of the morning
languishing between dream and waking I was standing with
two other people and suddenly one became vividly distinct.
It was Jack our senior engineer who I hadn't seen for some
years. He was in vivid Technicolor and beamed at me as I
jokingly said, "Who is this?" That amazing image has stuck
in my mind and the wonderful feeling of the reality of the
other side. The same year in the early dozing waking hours
my mother-in-law and an unknown lady shuffled quickly
around the bed and I knew she was going to hug me and I
thought to myself how is this going to work. The first time
she wore a long white nightie-like dress at another time she
was at the back door in ordinary clothes. It is this blending
of realities that is the hardest concept to come to terms with
for even in this world, which is pretty much bound by the
laws of Physics, there are strange, sometimes multiple,
coincidences which can have a dream-like quality.
Most of us assume that we are awake because we remember
getting out of bed. Our dreams are not so real therefore we
can draw the distinction between waking and sleeping but

Page 78

how can we ever be sure that we are truly awake? What if this is the dream and at least some of our dreams are a glimpse of reality. Some do claim that their dreams are almost like another life but if you believe that the mind is purely a product of the brain it's silly to even suggest that dreams can actually be true experiences, the obvious answer must be that they only seem to be real at the time. If, however, the human body is a mere puppet animated by mind then the mind might leave the body and have experiences in other places in other dimensions. One man dreamed he was inside a machine at work and was able to identify a fault that had cost the company a lot of money. Some researchers have been able to become aware during a dream and therefore make decisions. Their awareness became much greater and I assume their ability to bring the memory back was increased: I have been able to do that to the extent that I could change a disturbing plot. Some of these adventurers have recorded their experiences so that we might have a glimpse of something real or is it imagined? Let us try to understand what it is that survives: Is it will-o-the wisp or something with which we can identify?

OUT OF THE BODY

Dr Raymond Moody realised that he was hearing stories that had striking similarities from many different people; he eventually published them in his book, *'Life After Life.'* (Corgi 1975.) An ordinary no-nonsense down-to-earth person, who has always assumed that death is the end, is involved in an horrific car crash and finds himself up in the air watching peacefully as firemen cut his body from the tangled wreckage. In some cases the unseen observer hears no words and is only able to pick up the thoughts of the rescue teams. Sometimes the arriving ambulance men walk through the victim completely unaware of his presence.

In the operating theatre the patient rises up to the ceiling next to the clock looking down upon the nurses and doctors as they try to save the dying body. The patient can also see and hear everything that is said and done by grieving relatives in another part of the hospital.

He may then find himself travelling rapidly down a long dark tunnel. (This tunnel reminds me of the current idea put forward by Physicists that there are wormholes in space - tunnels that transcend time and space.) He moves towards a brilliant light and into a world where there are friends and relatives who speak without words. The people and the places seem to glow with an inner light, the atmosphere being one of total love. Many meet a being that seems to be composed of pure light. The religious sometimes *assume* that this is God, Jesus, Mohammed, Krishna, Buddha, Diva or Shiva, depending upon their upbringing. This being of light prompts a review of the whole of the person's life in a vividly-real panoramic view. This includes the thoughts and reactions of other people and there is an acute awareness of the embarrassing and unsavoury episodes. But the being of light looks on with humour and understanding and prompts the questions, 'What have you done with your life and what have you learned?' At this point he may be given the choice whether to go or to stay, a bridge or gate sometimes symbolises a point of no return. One lady saw an old fashioned telephone box pressing button B would return her to her body. Thoughts of a wife struggling on alone or of children left to fend for themselves drew one man back to the body. Another lady even came back because her husband wouldn't know how to iron his shirts!

On their return there is absolutely no loss of consciousness but once again they have to face the pain from which for a while they have been free and some are quite angry that the doctors have brought them back. All maintain that the experience was hyper real; more real, and more vivid, than ordinary everyday life and they will never again fear death. Sceptical medical staff and relatives have to think again because the patient has obviously witnessed things he/she couldn't possibly have seen or heard, especially at a time when that individual may have been certified brain dead.

Could OBE's be caused by drugs or the peculiar state of the brain at such a moment? Doctor Raymond Moody has examined all other options and found them wanting. With NDE's the popular view held by many doctors and psychiatrists is that the effect is caused either by lack of oxygen or chemicals generated in the dying brain.

(Life After Life Dr Raymond Moody.Jr MD. Corgi.)

According to Dr Melvin Morse there is no evidence to support this idea: 37 children were interviewed *'who had been treated with almost every type of mind-altering medication'* ... *'none of them had anything resembling a near-death experience.'*

(P23. 'Closer to The Light.' Melvin Morse MD with Paul Perry. Bantam Books. 1991.)

During OBE and NDE subjects, blind since birth, were not only able to see in vivid colours, <u>they could both recognise and had the words to describe who and what they saw:</u> This was totally different to their dreams in which they were still blind.   ('Mindsight.' Kenneth Ring and Sharon Cooper. I Universe 2008.)

One may wonder how the mind can exist without a body, the answer is at conception a back up file is created atom for atom like two gasses in the same space we have a duplicate body attached by an umbilical cord which can stretch to infinite lengths.

William Gerhardi wrote *'And in turning I became aware for the first time of a strange appendage. At the back of me was a coil of light, like a luminous garden hose resembling the strong broad ray of dusty light at the back of a dark cinema projecting onto the screen in front. To my utter astonishment that broad cable of light at the back of me illuminated the face on the pillow, as if attached to the brow of the sleeper. The sleeper was myself, not dead, but breathing peacefully, my mouth slightly open ... and here I was outside it, watching with a thrill of joy and fear.'*

('Man outside Himself' P45 Prevost Battersby. Psychic Book Club 1943.)

Countless dreamers populate the region near to the earth's vibrations called the 'Astral.' *Now and again a real astral dweller would appear without the silver cord of the dreamers. These cords never got tangled and could pass through each other quite easily. ...'*

(P160. 'Gone West.' J.S.M.Ward. BA Cambridge. Trance-vision, auto writing.
Ryder. 1918)

And there we are, no missing parts no wrinkles and the mind can exist as a consciousness in space with all-round vision and communication by telepathy. The spiritual body seems to be whatever the consciousness or unconscious mind dictates whether it is an eye in space, a ball or some other shape or shadow. One woman tried to wake her husband but had *'no hands to shake or touch him,* (she said) *there was nothing of me.'*..(P97 You Cannot Die. Ian Curie. Hamlyn. 1978)

During his first OBE Radio broadcasting executive Robert Monroe reached toward the wall without even realising that his arm had stretched to twice its normal length. He wrote that the 'non-physical body ' is like jelly that *"remembers the human form"* and the memory can become weaker until it assumes just *'a ball'...'or a blob.'* He suggested *'slipping out of the second body'* just *'after separation'* adding *'you can always "grow" a hand and an arm if you need one'*

(P296. Far Journeys. Robert Monroe Doubleday 1985)

Page 82

As we each of us have had countless lives (More about this later) we have had numerous personalities each with a different body therefore we can appear to our loved ones as they remember us. This is apparent with spirit guides who may be a relative. They may use a persona which is suitable for the work they do or to capture the medium's imagination. Maurice Barbanell's guide 'Silver Birch,' famous for his wonderful philosophy, used the astral body of a Red Indian likewise children can be much older souls than their squeaky voice suggests.

Subjects hypnotically regressed to their life in the spirit world saw spirits as lights or 'eyes and shapes which turn into people.' (This sounds similar to people who often see faces as they close their eyes at night.)

(P32. 'Journey of Souls.' Llewellyn Publications. 1997.)

When my sister suffered from Iritus and was temporarily blind she saw all kinds of frightening things – ravines and birds but also mam and dad sitting on the settee. These are assumed to be hallucinations known as Charles Bonnet Syndrome (CBS) Perhaps as in meditation or mediumship they are a mixture of spiritual sight, hallucination and memory. When clairvoyants concentrate upon their inner mind or certain objects including crystal balls, tea leaves, the wall paper even, the mind combines the pattern with the memory to form new images presented through the subconscious.

In the spirit world even spectacles, walking sticks and jewellery may be reproduced though damage to the physical body might not. Muldoon and Carrington include the case of a Mr. Slater who, after leaving the body, was surprised to find that a 'bad cut 'on his hand was not there.'

(P192 'The Phenomena of Astral Projection.' Muldoon & Carrington. Rider 1969.)

Waldo Vieira, M. D. thought about his son's superman cape and it immediately appeared on his back (P54.) He says that 'thinking, wishing and acting occur simultaneously.' (P167)

('Projections of the Consciousness.' Waldo Vieira, M. D
International Institute of Projectiology& Conscientiology. 1997.)

This is a frightening thought as I imagine few people make it a habit to control their own minds and so life out of the body could be quite bewildering. Generally speaking many people seem to report a feeling of immense well being and don't want to return to the body. Whilst normally under the direction of the subconscious mind an act of will can alter the appearance if so desired. It is understandable that the more malleable body will show more of one's emotions, what is surprising is that even clothing and accessories also reflect the inner man thus on the darker planes a man who would be king wore a rusty crown and a rusty sword.

Some of those who found themselves out of the body took great pains to verify the reality of their experience for example by appearing to friends miles away and being able to relate events in the operating theatre during a period when they were medically dead. Since Doctor Raymond Moody's *'Life After Life,'* was published we have had the film, *'Ghost,'* in which the individual is shown larger than life after being stabbed. This no doubt inspired a British road safety campaign with the victim being killed in a car accident, then the camera shows him as he realises that he is looking at his own dead body. There is the finality of it all being suddenly cut off from loved ones and feeling totally helpless, unable to intervene further in the continuing drama. These graphic representations help us to visualise the possibility of existing outside the body. In actual fact the near-death subjects rarely want to come back but those who leave the body in less life-threatening circumstances may feel a mixture of normal human emotions such as fear of the unknown. Waldo Vieira, able to leave the body at will since the age of nine, says that if all troubled individuals could have just one lucid out-of-body experience the world would be a better place.

(P179. 'Projections of the Consciousness.'
International Institute of Projectiology and Conscientiology. 1997.)

There are many cases where an individual is suddenly looking down on his or her own body still performing an ordinary task such as going into a shop and purchasing something; a nurse at an operating table or a musician playing the organ. In a body that is virtually weightless there is a tremendous feeling of well being, especially when the physical body is not in good condition.

One 78 years old lady said, *'I was now fully aware of myself as being a superior spiritual being and of far superior quality than my temporary self below.' ... 'I floated down the staircase ... only just able to touch the banister rail occasionally with the tips of my fingers, and not feeling any stairs beneath my feet. I came to earth in the hall, went out into the sunshine and skipped and danced on the gravel with a joyous sense of God that has survived all the years between.'* (px. Casebook of Astral Projection. Dr Robert Crookall. Citadel. 1980.)

You can *"soar... fly, drift, hover, spin, walk on water, tiptoe on the leaves of a towering tree, breath under the waves as you swim.* (P56 Marlene Druhan. 'Naked Soul' Llewellyn 1998)

Waldo Vieira could see *'around every side and in all directions at once'* ... *'a block of flats like 'a skeleton of the building...illuminated and inhabited - very much like a China cabinet.'*
(P44/5. Projections of the Consciousness by Waldo Vieira.
International Institute of Projectiology and Conscientiology. 1997.)

The False Awakening:- On several occasions Oliver Fox thought he was wide-awake rather like the school girl in *'Dreams'* only to reawaken some moments later. Once, in an attempt to prove to his wife that they were both out of the body, he jumped out of the window, an act that required some courage. He floated down to the pavement and the instant his feet touched it he was awake in bed. He was never able to tell if these incidents were a creation of his own mind or whether his wife was 'fun*ctioning in her astral vehicle.'* His wife had no memory of the incident whatsoever. (P69/70.)

On another occasion everything appears so normal and yet he notices in the lounge *'an oriental lacquer cabinet'* which is not there in real life. A parrot flies through the wall and again his wife seems to be a part of the illusion. (P115.)   (Astral Projection. Rider. 1920)

At the 7th Mind and Body Symposium held at the Institute of Psychiatry, Dr. Max Velmans from Goldsmiths University, London, *'quoted the case of a man who ... found himself looking down on his body laying on a bed. He tried to re-enter his body but could not. In desperation, and in order to force the issue, he decided to throw his projected body out of the 3rd floor window. Unfortunately he made the wrong decision and woke up later in hospital.'*

(Lew Sutton. 'Psychic News.' November 16th 1996.)

Vincent Turvey says that in plain long-distant clairvoyance, *"I appear to see through a tunnel which is cut through all intervening physical objects, such as towns, forests and mountains. This tunnel seems to terminate just inside Mr Brown's study, for instance, and I can only see what is actually there, and am not able to walk about the house, or use any other faculty but that of sight. In fact, it is almost like extended physical sight on a flat earth void of obstacles.*

"In Mental-body-travelling ... the 'I' appears to leave the 'Me' and to fly through space at a velocity which renders the view of the country over which 'I' pass very indistinct and blurred. The 'I' appears to be about two miles above the earth, and can only barely distinguish water from land, or forest from city; and only then if the tracts perceived be fairly large in area. Small rivers or villages would not be distinguishable. When I arrive at Mr. Brown's house in Bedford. 'I' am not only able to see into one room, but am able to walk about the house, see the contents of various rooms, and boxes, touch the curtain, and feel that it is made of velvet, move a table or bed, smell an escape of gas, diagnose a disease, look into the 'surroundings' of Mr. Brown, and, in a few cases, 'I' have been visible. 'I' also hear parts of conversations; and on several occasions 'I' have controlled a medium, and introduced myself through

his organism to people present, and have carried on a conversation with them."

(P93. 'Man Outside Himself.' Prevost Battersby. Psychic Book Club. 1943.)

The following story from Yram beautifully illustrates the interaction which may take place between the living and the 'dead' or in this case the living and the living:-

"I had used my ability to travel in the fourth dimension in order to pay periodical visits to a young woman who, later on, became my wife. After we had met three or four times on the physical plane, circumstances intervened to separate us, one from the other, by several hundreds of miles. It was then that, without knowing either the town or the house where she was living, I used to go to her every night by means of self projection, and it was whilst in this state that we became engaged ... My fiancé' was able to confirm by letter the exactness of the details about which I wrote ... She would feel my presence and speak to me, mentally, without being able to see me. "Whatever might be the place where she happened to be, whatever she might be doing, she would immediately have the very definite feeling that I was near her, and, if her attention was engaged, she would ask me to come again a little later ... She had the sensation of finding herself near a focus of energy from which she constantly received waves of great intensity. She was able to perceive my thoughts as easily as I could receive hers. "One day, when I was projected in the astral and standing beside her, she said: ' Stay near me!' 'Instead of that, 'I rejoined, 'you come with me.' Immediately, freeing herself from her physical body, she joined me. Later on, after we were married, it often happened that we would travel together in space, with a sweetness of sensation impossible to describe. "her love penetrated into my being under the guise of a general warmth, while a feeling of absolute confidence filled my spirit. On the other hand, my aura penetrated into hers and I had the sensation as if melting into her ... In no other experience have I had so wide-awake

a consciousness, no love so powerful, nor a calm and serenity so profound."
(P90/1 'Man Outside Himself.' Prevost Battersby. Psychic Book Club. 1943.)

Whilst these travellers cannot, like Gulliver, bring back a tiny sheep to prove that they have really been in another world, their stories will help us to set the scene on our journey through strange and enchanted lands. The interaction between the two sides of existence seems to be more common than we realise. There is the unseen, unfelt interaction of mind upon mind, also feelings and moments when the 'dead' can be seen and even touched: For a brief period they seem to be more in our world than in their own. Some writers describe a busy life of service whilst out of the body during sleep both to the living and the newly passed over. Waldo Vieira describes groups working in great cities with individuals that have every kind of problem including *'despair,' 'sadness'* and *'loneliness.'* Some have already passed over and a few of them refuse the help that is offered. The helpers have links with *'Police Stations,' 'The Salvation Army,' 'Alcoholics Anonymous'* and various other *'physical crisis control groups.'* (P28.)
(P70. Projections of the Consciousness. Waldo Vieira, M.D. ASPR. SPR. International Institute for Projectiology and Conscientiology. (IIPC.) 1997.)

Robert Alvery describes a meeting where the sleepers suddenly disappear from the room as they wake up:
(P30 Out of the body experiences. Robert Alvery. Regency Press. 1975.)

Others help those who have passed over in disasters for example still believing that they are alive but trapped under a collapsed building. (Bruce Moen. 'Voyage beyond Doubt.' Hampton Roads)

We have seen something of our world as it might appear to them; let us now try to catch a glimpse of their world through those who have eyes to see.

THE FINAL OOBE.

Woody Allen summed up the popular view of death when he said,
"I don't mind dying. I just don't wanna be around when it happens."
Perhaps the truth of the matter was more clearly stated by Winston Churchill when he said something like; "Death is only an incident and not the most important which happens to us in this state of being!"

Those who think that the person *is* the body are naturally fearful of anything that reminds them that one day it will wear out and simply stop functioning like any other machine. At home the subject of death was usually referred to as 'if anything happens to....' Some people are even prepared to take out a second mortgage in order that their severed head or whole body if they are rich can be preserved until the day that science can breathe new life into old. If the spirit body is indeed a reality the practise of cryogenics looks like a sick joke for even if it were possible, who in their right mind would want to return from a world of beauty to become a living Frankenstein in a world of strangers? But I wonder if the body can be repaired would a spirit enter into it; would it be the original owner or something more sinister desperate to get back into the world.
Death heralds thoughts of coffins, cemeteries, graves, cremations and the clinging on to the last few years of life, always uncertain when the grim reaper will come. All too often thoughts of the future are negative and rarely does a person look upon death as the gateway to a new and exciting life with the interval in between an opportunity to fill the last few years on earth with achievement, cheerfulness and hope: Little wonder as bereavement and illness can devastate the most positive of persons. Though many an ailing and weary soul does look upon death as a merciful release, ideally we should take the opportunity to balance the books before we go. We should show those

around us how much we love and value them and try to compensate for our past mistakes by helping, even if only with a sympathetic ear and the voice of experience. In other words we should treat each day as our last because death is something we experience every time we go to sleep. - It is the final OBE! It is said that birth is a tragedy and death is the happiest day of your life.

Even the suffering can cling onto life for fear of death and perhaps we all worry about how we will go but the truth is we can suffer not to die but to recover our health and happiness. We can also die peacefully in our sleep without any suffering; the two things are not necessarily related.

Dr Osis, speaking on TV, said that he was impressed by the way the face of the dying would light up. He suggested that the average person wouldn't feel too happy if he or she suddenly came face to face with a terrorist holding a machine gun because the natural inclination is for a human being to cling to life at all costs.

Sometimes the dying claim to have met someone who had unbeknown to them died perhaps in the same accident. Many Doctors and nurses have noticed that just before dying, pain and mental confusion can sometimes subside and the patient becomes calm and lucid.

One *'doctor reported that a 22 year old man who had been blind all of his life, suddenly, in the minutes before his death, glanced around the room, smiling, apparently seeing doctors and nurses, and for the first time, members of his family.'* (P24. 'Death Encounters,' Fiore-Landsburg. Bantam. 1979.)

During a tragedy teams of helpers will be present when many of the injured are not aware that they are 'dead' and still imagine themselves trapped. Those who do meet a horrific ending it would seem have left the body and may indeed be observing the event in a state of peaceful curiosity. The near-death experience seems to be telling us that the pain is often not registered by the dying who have thrown off the tattered old overcoat and are busy meeting loved ones after perhaps years of wearisome loneliness. Mr Biggs, one of Leslie Flint's voices told his story,

After the Doctor had gone they came for the body. *They slumped it down like an old sack of potatoes. I thought, "I'm not going after them. I'm going to sit here in my home. I might as well sit down in my chair now it's empty. "So I sat down and tried to think it all out ... 'All of a sudden it was just as if the fireplace disappeared and I could see beautiful green fields and trees, and a little sort of - I was going to say river but it was more like a brook. And I could see something - at first I didn't know what it was coming towards me in the distance. I made it out it was a figure. It was my mother!*

'Dear oh dear. She looked, oh as I'd seen her in the picture which I'd still got in the room hanging up on the wall - my mother when she was first married. She came right up what was the fireplace towards me, and she was smiling all over her face, as happy as a sand boy. '"Come one," she says, you don't want to stay here. It's no good sitting here. No one's going to take any notice of you. May won't realise, you know. You have to come and be with me." 'It was funny,' said Mr Biggs, 'going through what had been my fireplace into this lovely sort of countryside. As we was walking my mother was nattering away to me telling me all sorts of things ... funny thing was she wasn't opening her mouth.'

(*'Life After Death.'* P52. Neville Randall. Direct Voice. Medium Leslie Flint. Corgi. 1975.)

Roads which lead out of the fireplace seem to have more in common with 'Alice through the looking glass' than reality and yet the 'near-deathers' report exactly the same kind of experience: the blending of one reality with another. The theory is that there is no actual distance between one dimension and the next the difference being merely one of frequency or vibration. As the spirit gradually separates from the body many of the dying are able to see into that other world. The screen is removed to reveal something of what lies behind the scenes, the camera draws back and we see the producer, technicians and actors temporarily out of the action: Far from the horror that we all might imagine we have woken from the dream, escaped from the prison house and we are free.

And when we see them and they see us they glow; the happiness the ecstasy is so overwhelming but the pain is soon forgotten. (2019)

The shortness of the time we have with each other does nothing to lessen the pain and it is often the unexpectedness of it which is so traumatic, even though we might stop breathing at any minute. After a whole lifetime of living together a part of us is wrenched away and yet it takes only days to forge this bond. How can anybody possibly cope when in place of a beautiful warm baby they find a "lifeless polystyrene doll?"

Do you remember what it was to return home? To mark the empty chair, the vacated bed, the familiar possessions left behind; and to feel that the dear arms would never twine round your neck again; that the voice you loved to listen to was silenced for ever; that the eyes you gazed in with delight were closed and dull; that your child had left you; that he was lying in his narrow coffin under the cruel sods, out in the cold and the frost and the rain, and you would see him never more until you had passed through the dread mystery yourself? Did you not lie awake at night, sobbing instead of sleeping, peering with your inflamed eyes into the impenetrable darkness yearning for the "touch of a vanished hand, and the sound of a voice that was still;" feeling that you would give anything and dare anything only to hear one word, to see one glimpse that would convince you that your beloved had not gone utterly beyond the reach of your affection and your tears?

(P27-8. 'The Spirit World.' Florence Marryat. F.V.White. 1896.)

The first time I met Derek was after his demonstration when I discovered that he too was a television engineer so I invited him home for a cuppa. 'Has Ann had a miscarriage' he asked me. 'There's a thirteen years old boy standing behind her.' Thirteen years previously Ann had miscarried she didn't know she was pregnant at the time. Apparently foetuses grow up in the spirit world so there will be a lot of extra family members waiting to greet us when we get there.

R. J. Lees is told of a home for children which consisted of *'a surprising number of palatial buildings'* including a *'pre-natal'* nursery, *dormitories, gymnasium, museum, theatre, laboratory and other places answering to every possible demand which may arise.... A system of landscape gardening appeared to be designed to prompt questions.* (P96.)... ... *The object of every such institution is to foster enquiry in the minds of the children.*

(The Life Elysian. R. J. Lees. 1905. Wm. Cross, Leicester. 1953.)

One man had an OBE during a diabetic coma and met his sister who was dying in another part of the hospital. *'...she kept telling me to stay where I was, "It's not your time," she said. Then she just began to recede off into the distance through a tunnel while I was left there alone.'* On his return the doctor at first denied that she had died.' *he had a nurse check on it. She had in fact died just as I knew she did.'*

(P136. 'The Light Beyond.' Raymond Moody Jr. Pan Books. 1988.)

I suppose those who imagine a heaven cannot conceive of a real place populated by real people it literally sounds too good to be true; a fairy tale; echoes of our primitive past. There are many events in life which can feel surreal, things that only happen to other people which may be horrible or on the other hand even a dream come true. Many of us might think it is better to be skeptical or pessimistic so if there really is nothing after death we won't be disappointed and I guess there's some logic in there somewhere. Maybe it's better to be optimistic and hope for the best but that would be foolish, to imagine that there are houses and streets in the sky is ridiculous. I remember a scientist on a TV discussion program saying that if there was a place like that the astronauts would have seen it. Whilst the spiritual worlds might have all of the qualities of a dream we are told that the vivid reality of the place makes life on earth look like a dream. The following was dictated to the famous Victorian medium, R. J. Lees by his spirit friend who stood beside him.

I heard a scream, and saw a child in deadly peril among the horses in the road. He was not far away, so bounding foreword-with no thought but for his safety - I reached and dragged him from his hazardous position, then turned, and-Something touched me. I clasped the boy more firmly and stepped forward. The noise ceased, vehicles and street faded away, as if some great magician had waved his wand, the darkness disappeared, and I was lying upon a grassy slope in an enchanted land. Neither did all the changes lie in our surroundings. Few people would have been enamoured of the ragged child I rushed to save, with his shoeless feet, matted hair and unwashed face; but the angel I found lying on my breast would have driven an artist into raptures. For myself, in that instant, I had changed my morning suit for a loosely flowing robe which somehow appeared to be a part of myself;'

I was reclining on the grass of what can only be described as the auditorium of an immense but natural amphitheatre with the arena occupied by a multitude who appeared to be engaged in the reception of strangers, whom they were welcoming and congratulating.... There were two classes of persons represented - the one, evidently residents, attired in garments embracing almost every shade of colour with which I was familiar, and some the like of which I had never seen before, and therefore have no means to make you understand. The other, by far the smaller of the two, gave me the idea of strangers, who having just arrived, stood in need of the help and assistance so freely proffered...'

'Before me lay a plain, across which numbers were continually coming and going; at its further side I saw a heavy bank of fog laying. ... I was conscious of a cold chill

running through me, ... such as one experiences at the thought of leaving a cosy fire to become enveloped in the piercing mist of autumn of early winter. What caused this is more than I can say-perhaps it was sympathy with those I saw emerging from such surroundings; for many were so overcome they scarcely had the strength to reach the open plain; while for some the watchers plunged into the mists and carried them through; others being borne all the way across the plain before they had the power to stand upon their feet.' (P17/18/19.)

' ... I turned, and saw a young woman clad in the daintiest of pink robes, coming down the hill towards me. I was not so sure, but thought her face bore a resemblance to one I had known in the long ago, except that the old furrows of care and want had been transformed into lines and curves of beauty. I had long since forgotten her, but she remembered me, and with eyes brilliant with welcome, and hands extended to clasp my own, she was the first of all I knew to greet me. (P24. 'Through The Mists.')

A PRISMATIC LANDSCAPE. - 'We reached the summit of the slope and I stood entranced by the scene which lay before me. From the foot of a gentle declivity, clothed in grass of the richest, softest green I had ever beheld, a landscape stretched away on every side dressed in more shades of colour than I had power to estimate. ... Pulsation's of visible vitality throbbed and trembled in stone, tree and flower. From the foot of the hill on which I stood, hundred paths diverged to every part of the landscape, not the monotonous prosaic roads to which earth is so accustomed, but every-one had not a name, but a distinctive colour corresponding with the city or district to which it lead. They were arranged so that the darker shades curved themselves on either hand in the foreground, each having a greater or lesser depression according to its tone until I lost them as they sank beneath my feet; the lighter tints appeared to have a corresponding elevation, until in the centre of the prospect lay one straight line of faultless white leading to an arc of brilliant purity in the far distance. ... I perceived that each person took the road corresponding in colour to the dress they wore.'

(P35. 'Through the Mists.')

'I grew momentarily more interested in my new and overpowering surroundings as every fresh thought and scene impressed itself upon me. ... Every single incident with which I became acquainted appeared to self-contain a heaven, and more of it than I had had power to imagine on earth. ...' *'Husband and wife, parent and child, brother and sister, friend and friends meeting after intervals more or less prolonged ... eyes on earth sightless, now feasted their hungry vision upon those who had guided them in their darkness; ears strained to listen to a mother's voice were now entranced with the sweetness of that music; tongues long silent poured forth their gratitude; and arms which had been powerless, closed in the rapt embrace of love.* (P42/43. 'Through The Mists.' Robert James Lees Trust.)

'In the distance lay a plain of apparently illimitable proportions, undulating and picturesque beyond description, in which hill and dale, lake and stream, terrace and plateau, park and pasture, grove and garden, city and homestead, palace and mansion, were so arranged and disposed as to contribute their own peculiar feature to the grandeur of the whole. Throughout that vast domain, each shrub and flower, each house and hill, each stream and lake had its legitimate balance to maintain in the general harmony; and wonderfully beautifully produced in the accomplishment of the design. ... Yet this was not heaven itself, but only one of the first halting places ... where homeward bound souls could rest and refresh themselves in their migration from the earth towards their Father's house of many mansions. ' (P53. Through the Mists)

'... language fails me to express the quality of the scene unfolded to my view ... from the foreground to the far-away horizon I could plainly see in that hazeless atmosphere of eternity, not only the effects in aggregate but the component

parts of each feature which in turn arrested my attention. Did I say it had its plains and streams? It were far more true to say my eye wandered over vast continents, fruitful and picturesque, each bounded by proportionate seas and oceans, from the poetic billows of which the sting of all destruction had been torn away. Mansion and palace gleamed resplendent in the shadowless sunlight, not cramped or circumscribed in detail or design, to suit the exigency of space or limit - not robbed of grace or beauty by the use of coarse material having the power to resist the storm and tempest...what need of such restrictions in the domain of the infinite, that kingdom where they refuse to traffic in the merchandise of tempest or decay. Each habitation had its terraces and crescents, gardens and quadrangles, all its own in such noble and magnificent proportions that its vision may have made to sleeping Nimrod the first suggestion of the royal and stately Babylon. The spiritual quarries from which coral and marble, porphyry and alabaster, malachite and jasper had been cast out as coarse and valueless, furnished the substance for each edifice, while the garniture was worked in multiform mosaics of diamond and sapphire, carbuncle and beryl, pearl and ruby, amethyst and emerald relieved by gems of tint and lustre earth has never seen. The carvings were the work of sculptors who wore rich the mantle of perfect inspiration... The gardens of old Babylon were forgotten in the contemplation of such horticultural attainments...' (P54.) ('Through the Mists.' *'Aphraar'* through R.J.Lees. 1898.

R.J.L.Trust. 7 Hensbury Gardens. Evington. Leics.)

The product of a vivid imagination you might think. According to Fredrick Sculthorpe, a constant Out-of-body traveller:-

'The lower and intermediate states appear to be vast zones of vibrations, split up like radio wave-bands into the tendencies, habits, or desires of the inhabitants, and are as numerous as only the infinite variety of minds can be.'
They vary in brightness from the lower dull states to the

'higher and brighter vibrations, the latter resembling a bright sunny day on earth.' (P107)

On the lower planes <u>the thoughts of the people there produce</u> *'a sickening harshness which is indescribable. The most depressing moments on earth cannot compare with it.'*
(Fredrick Sculthorpe. P37. 'Excursions to the Spirit World.' Greater World. 1961.)

In your world we have many challenges in our world we are called to account to add up, collate, analyse, all that we have done on earth that we may learn and be wiser from it. Where we have not stepped up to the mark perhaps we might have another go at it or at least rationalise it so that the lesson is learned and we can move on. Sometimes we do this by helping someone else in the same situation. You have many helpers; all of them have experiences of different worlds; different fashions; different outlooks; different requirements; hardships and fortunes. (December 2019.)

William Buhlman writes, *'non-physical cities and structures... continue to be moulded by the group consciousness of millions of non-physical inhabitants. When we enter these environments our thoughts will not change the structures encountered.'*

'A nonconsensus environment ... is not firmly moulded by a group ... The appearance can be anything we imagine: a forest, a park, a city, an ocean, even an entire planet ... while often physical-like in appearance, they are extremely sensitive to focused thoughts and will rapidly change and restructure according to the prevailing conscious and sub-conscious thoughts present in the immediate area. ...

Nonconcensus areas are often moulded by our subconscious mind for our benefit ... often confronting ((our)) greatest fears and limits. For example, if you are deathly afraid of heights, you could experience yourself climbing a mountain or crossing a narrow bridge.'

'Natural (raw) energy environments ... appear without a specific shape or form ... often observed as misty voids, empty space, or featureless, open areas ... of white, silver,

or golden clouds of energy.' 'No matter what dimension we inhabit, our personal responsibility for our thoughts and actions is absolute.' 'This is why spiritual leaders have always stressed themes of "do unto others" and "love for all."' (P95. 'Adventures Beyond the Body.' William Buhlman, Hale. 1996.)

Frederick Sculthorpe gives some of the best descriptions of the earth-like planes, they convey a feeling of normality: a busy world full of people doing most of the things which contribute to a happy and interesting life such as visiting each other's homes where he notices that some of the house names on the wooden gates showed faint impressions of the names used by the previous occupiers. (P73.) In the shopping centres, arcades and tearooms no money changes hands. Some are happy to serve in these shops whilst others give service in their own sphere of interest. There are furnishing, clothing, hardware and apartment stores where some of the goods displayed have been designed simply for the pleasure of seeing an idea take shape. He describes well-stocked butcher's shops in a land where the slaughter of animals is not possible. Thought had simply created the meat that corresponded to the butcher's idea of it rather than the real thing because it was a brilliant red and in one case almost a crimson colour. (P40.) There is sightseeing and whilst one expects to see lovely gardens and landscapes there are also rivers, boats; sandy beaches and seasides. He even describes a coach ride and road traffic which included many homemade constructions the like of which he says would never move an inch on earth. Some places seem to be a reflection of earth, towns with buildings not yet built yet also places as they were many years ago. Some towns had factories where people seemed to working away believing they were still alive there were also tea rooms and streets. He tells us that everything is reproduced down to the smallest detail. *'There are even street lamps in a world where no artificial light is necessary.'* His wife once came down to him from a higher plane where they met in the park. He said that when he was taken by his teacher *'through the people and the closed door this always surprises me in the lower planes because I never know when I am invisible.'*

(Fredrick Sculthorpe P42. 'Excursions to The Spirit World.' Greater World.)

In Anthony Borgia's book there is a fascinating description of the building of an addition to the library. After the planning has been completed, architects and masons gather round together with the chief of that region and in response to a prayer, a beam of light appears which slowly materialises and solidifies the building.

('Life in the World Unseen.' P151. Anthony Borgia Two Worlds. 1954.)

Seventeen years old *'Mike Swain,'* speaking to his father through trance medium Nina Merrington described how he cruised above the ground until he found a spot that tickled his fancy. *'The architects'...'visualised, in their minds, the type of house that would suit me best. Then the builders arrived...'and "...the shimmering outlines of my house began to appear!"* (P40.) He illustrated the difficulty of creative visualisation for example if he wanted a new Rolls Royce he would have to imagine it in three dimensions with every detail correct. Merely imagining a picture of a Rolls would produce just that. He says, *"Whenever I need to feel the refreshing rain beating in my face, and the wind blowing my head clear, I go into an open field and I think - and then I enjoy my own private thunderstorm." ... "The rain forms little puddles as I walk; yet when I turn round and look behind me, there's no sign of it - only the usual long green grass."*

('From My World to Yours.' P41. Jasper Swain. Nina Merrington. Walker & Co. 1977.)

'Joe' says that ...*'There are things ... of the same kind as you see on earth, only somehow different. They are real, but you have a sense that they are only temporary ... Then you find, and it seems very curious and fascinating, that you can change those things by wishing them to change. You can only do it with quite small and unimportant things, but for instance-you can look at a pine needle on the ground ... and begin to think of it as a real needle, a steel*

needle, and then it is an ordinary sewing needle and you can pick it up.'... 'You can't change the whole scene ... because ... it belongs to lots of other spirits too, but you can change any little thing, when the change won't affect anybody else. Then you begin to realise that all the things around you are really thought forms, and that it is arranged like that so as to make the transition easy from material to spirit life. You can learn a great deal simply by finding out what you can alter by changing your own thought about it, and what remains unaltered however you think about it.'

('Joe's' Scripts in - P74. 'Living On'. Paul Beard. Allen & Unwin. 1980.)

'Mike Swain' again:- "We have a lot of fun with the teenagers who have just arrived here. They think they're still the cat's whiskers. Oh Dad, you'd laugh to see them primping around as if they were in a department store, changing out of one set of glad rags to put on another, and then starting again from scratch and dreaming up something even more weird and wonderful! Which promptly appears, as large as life and twice as natural! They have the time of their lives for hours!"

(P37. 'From My World to Yours.' Jasper Swain. Walker & Co. N.Y. 1977.)

One of the most interesting books I have read recently was transmitted through Brigitte Rix. Brigitte's *'mum'* found that when she went *'outside'* the scene would be at one time a *'street with shops or field or parks'* at others' *the countryside or a town.'* (P52. I'm Not Dead I'm Alive' Con Psy 2011)

Some describe thoughts that appear above the heads of individuals for example a piano materialised above the head of a pianist. One of the first things I remember being told by Sissy Simpson the first medium I ever met when I first took an interest in this subject was that "thoughts are living things." Whilst physical things fade away perhaps the memory is eternal.

Brigitte's *'mum'* says that one has to learn to control one's passing thoughts otherwise they keep *'appearing right and left.'* (P54.) She was admiring a rose in her garden when it suddenly *'appeared near'* her in a vase that she had *'never seen before.'* (P80.) The texture of a flower, for example, seems to be made up of droplets of light. She was told that *'the skin of things...is not made of atoms but rather of inside of atoms.* (I'm Not Dead.' P124. - Con-Psy. 2011.)

(Sir) *'Oliver Lodge'* through Raymond Smith says:-
'When thoughts of love are received from my wife, family & friends in other levels, I find that just by a thought I am with them in whatever environment is befitting to us.'... 'By the creative ability of our minds, my wife and I can meet in an etheric double of Mariemont, an earthly house in which we shared both the joys and problems of life. Everything that exists in any level of consciousness does so only by the creative ability of the minds of its inhabitants. We share one another's creations and, on arrival, add to them by the experiences we have brought with us.'
(P34. 'Nobody Wants to Listen - and Yet.' Raymond Smith Con Psy Pubs. 1995.)

Waldo Vieira, M.D., described a live scene that was projected by helpers at an institute. This included his mother, Waldo himself at a younger age and his son who he said had not yet been born. He tried to *'approach the very realistic images without success. The ephemeral forms dispersed just like vaporous plastic, gauze, tissue or foam rubber.'*
(P41. Projections of the Consciousness by Waldo Vieira, M.D.
International Institute of Projectiology and Conscientiology. 1997.)

Little wonder so many find it hard to believe that they are not dreaming:- The eyesight seems to be extended reaching crisp and clear into the far distance, some report a 360-degree vision. I imagine that what they see is a land not unlike the scenery depicted in a child's fairy book with light, colours, music and feelings combining to create a strange and wonderful experience: Flowers, trees, birds and animals are set in a wonderland more beautiful than any earthly scene yet containing all of the elements with which we are familiar; *'Beautiful bright meadows;'* *'Fields of yellow corn.' 'Deep blue skies.'* Streets and buildings that seem to be made of shining gold and silver. Brilliantly lit cities *'with domes and steeples in beautiful array';* grand country houses, charming cottages, woodland and gardens so exquisitely laid out that each scene is a feast for the eyes and the other senses too. *'Typical English gardens'...'Lush green velvety lawns bounded by deep curving borders, a riot of colour and fragrance.'* Seas, rivers, *crystalline streams,* mountains, hills and dales, all play their part in the composition of that magical land. There were people who seemed to be in shining clothes with a sort of glow and everywhere a beautiful shadow less light with feelings of love, peace and joy. And yet the places and the people are still within the bounds of the physical. Some writers describe places which to some are more heavenly like with all kinds of festivals .... During an OOBE, Dr. George Ritchie had a *'glimpse'* of a city *'constructed of light'* and the people there were *'blindingly bright.'*

(P148. 'Death Encounters.' Fiore/Landsburg. Bantam. 1979.)

'Monsignor Benson' through the hand of Anthony Borgia tells us that in each realm lives a ruler who is of a higher plane. These souls possess great experience and knowledge and are always available to those who bring their problems for solution: -

'His hair seemed to be as of bright golden light rather than the colour of gold. He looked to be young, to be of eternal youthfulness, but we could feel the countless aeons of time, as it is known on earth, that lay behind him. When he spoke his voice was sheer music, his laugh as a rippling of the waters, but never did I think it possible for one individual to breath forth such affection, such kindliness, such thoughtfulness and consideration; and never did I think it possible for one individual to possess such an immensity of knowledge as is possessed by this celestial king. One felt that, under the Father of Heaven, he held the key to all knowledge and wisdom. ...'

(P249. 'Life in the World Unseen.' Two Worlds Publishing. 1954.)

'This life which awaits you is not a mere bodiless dream in a twilight region somewhere beyond the real and the actual. No; it is filled with service and endeavours crowned, one after another with success; of patient pressing onward, and of indomitable wills attuned to each other in comrade service for the Lord of Love.

(P160. 'Life Beyond the Veil. 'Rev. Vale Owen. Greater World.)

This idealised very attractive world is perhaps what we all expect but realistically some who have had a gruelling life might need a period of adjustment. In the spirit world there are actually hospitals and doctors to heal the minds of those who have suffered a long and wearisome life.

It would appear that we leave the body during our sleeping hours but as the brain is asleep it doesn't retain the memories though I think sometimes it has a drowsy recollection of the experience. This means that terrifying thing called death is the final Out-of-Body experience; something we have done countless times. Generally speaking most people seem to feel an amazing release an overwhelming joy and certainly wouldn't want to come back to a worn-out weary body; but is it possible to pop back to say "I'm OK?"

...whenever we thought of our friends left behind we were aware of their pain, of their loss of their reaching out to us in the hope that we could hear them. ('*Friedrick.*' 6th August 2020)

Understandably we might decide to go a medium taking our carefully crafted evidence to prove that we are still alive and kicking. But the medium has a brain and a mind of her/his own which will question; interpret; even change the meaning and so the medium has to let the words pass through however weird or unlikely which is more difficult than you might think.

In spirit you are never at the end
You're always at the beginning.
'Veronica' (July 2020.)

MIND OVER MATTER.

When we first saw H.G.Wells', 'The Invisible Man,' it was a novel and exciting idea to see things moved about by unseen hands. Special effects have come a long way since those days making the old films look somewhat corny but when real objects start to fly about the house the effect can be quite frightening. Mind over matter is undoubtedly a fact, the question is, whose mind is doing the moving? To accept the idea of worlds beyond the senses that are to the inhabitants as concrete as the ground on which we walk we have to come to terms with the idea that our solidity may not be someone else's. Out-of-the-body travellers reported that this world of ours is but a shadow when looked at from the other side and we are the ghosts: What follows certainly seems to bear this out. While out of the body Eddie Slasher sometimes felt that people in the body could actually see him, even if it was perhaps only as a light.

(P39. 'Explorations out of the Body.' Kroshka Books. 1987.)

This was something I found when my colleague John died at 23. I was at home watching TV and I actually saw a patch of light twinkling above my head to the left. - If that makes any sense. – But I '*knew*' it was him laughing at me.

Robert Monroe described the time when he was out of the body and was able pinch a female business friend so hard that it caused her '*to jump a foot*' leaving her with brown and blue marks. Later she was astonished when Robert asked her if she remembered the pinch as she could see no one behind her at the time.

(P57. 'Journeys Out of the Body.' Robert Monroe. Dolphin. 1971.)

Back in Hydesville New York in 1848, a new craze was begun with the Fox sisters that was to spread to many Victorian drawing rooms in England. - 'Two raps for yes and one for no.' The sisters didn't understand what was happening to them and were the victims of both sceptics and crowds wanting to experience the spectacle of mediumship. Under more strictly controlled sittings leading

London researchers witnessed exceptional phenomena produced in the presence of Kate Fox. Many fraudsters found that this new phenomena could be faked and was quite lucrative making it even harder for genuine mediums to prove their case. For example the cameras of the day were so slow it was easy to replicate genuine ghost pictures with a bit of cotton wool to represent ectoplasm. Physical phenomena is looked upon as the lowest of the low amongst some Spiritualists as it is believed to attract spirits who will use the easiest method to put on a good show whist the medium is in trance completely unaware of the proceedings. Hence the mixture of fraud with the genuine especially if the medium has poor moral standards. Some genuine mediums were accused of cracking their toe joints to produce the sounds however cracking joints sound exactly…like cracking joints! Some of the raps in our circle were on the table undoubtedly spirit fingers being at one point those of a child and a female with long fingernails. Some raps can be as loud as a rifle shot; apparently genuine spirit raps end louder than they begin unlike normal raps that die away. At a lecture by northeast medium Stan Jones we heard a tape recording of the continuous loud rapping of a number of songs. During a circle held on Derek Cassidy's birthday, happy birthday was tapped out constantly during the three-hour sitting. Raps came from the ceiling, tables, chairs and other furniture in the room. Some years ago, as a visitor to Stan's circle held in a small dining room, I had been struck by the immense power which felt like a strong electric field and had the appearance of a heat haze. - I felt a hand touch mine whilst it was still light enough to see, I saw nothing. Sadie, whose house it was, was quite nervous and was often treated to noises but never when her daughter was in the room as she strongly objected to them. When Sadie told me this there was a loud clatter as 'someone' hit the hinged door on the lounge TV. Since that time I have been treated to lots of taps and scratches in our house over the years, though sometimes to distinguish from ordinary house noises I would ask for a response. I was told of one embarrassing incident where a 'medium' visiting a local church was standing next to a radiator, well known for pinging and gurgling. As it produced its usual clang the lady turned and said, "God bless." Those present had great difficulty in keeping a straight face and it was embarrassing however, misunderstandings are bound to happen. When things are moved around the house for example, it takes time and observation to be sure that we haven't just been absent-minded. Deep in thought one evening, I was treated to a very loud creak like a heavy footstep on the floor beside me. When I came down from the ceiling I rather ungraciously said, 'Don't ever do that again.' Since then taps and scratches have been noticeably absent. At one circle held in good light four of us had our finger tips touching the top of a small table which stood on one leg. This it continued to do as each in turn withdrew their fingers. When I was the only one touching the table it collapsed so whatever energy was causing the phenomenon I obviously hadn't got it. Sitters can sometimes feel pulling in the stomach area during some physical demonstrations; Stan often felt quite strong nausea.

During a lecture at the Hayes Centre, Swanwick, Author .Guy Lyon Playfair described one of the best-documented poltergeist cases that started August 1977 in a semi-detached council house in Enfield. The four children and their mother began to hear bangs, knockings and footsteps. Police, press, photographers, Guy Playfair and Maurice Grosse from the SPR, saw all manner of objects being moved including very heavy furniture. Toy bricks, marbles and even a book were 'thrown' sometimes through walls and ceilings, with a curved trajectory, arriving warm just like apports. The gas fire in the bedroom attached by an exceptionally hard metal pipe was torn out, the beds were upturned and two of the girls were often thrown out of bed but never hurt. (Though I believe at one point they may have been joining in with the fun and certainly looked almost giggly during an interview.) There was a feeling that somebody who couldn't be seen was there. Mrs Hodgson recalled the time she was cooking sausages when one jumped from the pan to the grill. *"It's almost as if someone is standing there with an invisible hand."* Both she and her daughter caught glimpses of a man also angry old men were heard shouting. When a VCR was being fitted in the bedroom a voice shouted, *"Get that machinery out of here."* Janet found a knife dancing around pointing at her and the light bulbs were always going. Interestingly, according to the eldest girl Rose, the phenomena did not cease when her sister Janet, the supposed source of the energy, was admitted to hospital (though a lot of activity occurred around and about her) but got worse when the divorced father visited.

(Guy Lyon Playfair. 'This House is Haunted.' Sphere 1980.)

Having attended the lecture and read accounts by sceptics there is still plenty of evidence which I think cannot be explained by teenage pranks and which fits in with well attested phenomena.

Professor Archie Roy was once told by a senior police officer that he had to take his men off a poltergeist case because they were putting reports in like, *'The bed was proceeding in a northerly direction.'* During a TV chat show one lady described gloves that boxed at her in mid-air. When asked how she reacted to this she laughed and said that she threw her wellies at them.

Matthew Manning's poltergeist phenomena began in the school dormitory. *'Heavy steel double-bunk beds moved of their own accord...Fourteen table knives of unknown origin were "thrown" against walls and beds',...*together with, amongst other things,... *'broken glass, nails and pebbles.'* Heat emanating from *'glowing lights'* that appeared on walls *'threatened to set the whole house on fire.'*

('The Link.' P44. Matthew Manning Corgi. 1974.)

Biologist, Dr. Lyall Watson, was spending an evening with a family in Venice. *'After dinner'* five-year- old Claudia picked up a tennis ball and *'stroked it'*...*'as though it were ... a door-mouse.'*...*'There was a short implosive sound, very soft like a cork being drawn in the dark and Claudia held in her hand something completely different ...'* an inside-out tennis ball. Watson, *'squeezed it ... bounced it'*, then, *'pierced the rubber and let the air hiss out.'* He cut it open and found the normal furry *'surface was inside.... Claudia... was able to repeat this amazing feat on other occasions.* (P20-21. 'Lifetide.' Lyall Watson. Coronet Books. 1979.)

In various laboratories there have been many studies on the ability of different individuals to affect by concentration; chemicals; a compass, levitate physical objects; bend metals or transfer healing energy. Nina Kalugina has *on some occasions* had remarkable results when she describes the feeling of *electricity rising up from her spine.* So intensely was her concentration at one time that she suffered a heart attack. These experiments, perhaps understandably generated an enormous amount of scepticism and hostility.
(The Probability of the Impossible Dr Thelma Moss. P125 1976 RKP)

In the July 1974 issue of 'Science of the Mind.' Dr Robert N. Miller reported experiments he had conducted with healer Olga Worrall who had placed her hands on either side of a cloud chamber used by nuclear physicists to detect high-energy particles. A strong wave pattern developed between them that always remained parallel to her hands even when she moved their position 90 degrees. This repeatable experiment was even achieved at a distance of 600 miles. *'Ingo Swan and two other subjects have also obtained similar results.'*
(P66. 'Photographing the Spirit World.' Cyril Permutt. Aquarian. 1983.)

In some countries so called holy men are reputed to perform all kinds of miracles including materialising precious objects; miraculous healing; being buried alive being in two places at once and so on. I must admit I am as sceptical about some of these claims as some are sure to be

Page 109

about the contents of this book. Whilst the function of a medium is not to perform party tricks the following demonstrates that some of them have extraordinary abilities. In trance the great medium D.D. Home was able to put his bushy hair into the *'bright wood fire'* and *'even place his face right among the burning coals, moving it about as though bathing it in water.'* On other occasions he was able to *'carry around glowing coal.'* William Crookes said that his *'soft and delicate skin'* ... *'showed* no trace of injury.' As if that wasn't enough Home placed a huge lump of burning coal on Mr Hall's head and drew the latter's white hair over it *'into a sort of pyramid.'*

(P167/8. The Paranormal. Brian Inglis. Paladin 1986.)

At Princeton University, subjects were shown mentally influencing the height of a computer-controlled water jet and the sound of a drum beat.

('The Paranormal World of Paul McKenna.' 19.2.96.)

Whatever mind is it is the expression of our consciousness and without it we wouldn't be aware that the universe exists. The basic structure of matter is light, virtually empty space in other words everything is based on electronic principles which opens up countless possibilities. We have seen the growth in electronic machines and gadgets in a relatively short time during which remote controls have been gradually evolving. What started with the pressing of buttons soon moved on to control first by wire then by ultrasonic sound followed by infra red: That is gradually giving way to voice commands: Attempts have been made to use the mind but that is still mechanical. When we use our brain to command the body to react; an implant or sensor watching the eye movement or detecting brain activity sends an electronic instruction to the gadget or the limb which then responds. Here we hit a brick wall when we have to ask what is it that commands the brain to act. Thought is a process which it seems is contained within the workings of the brain and associated with memory. But what is it that initiates the thought; we might call it the will but that gets us nowhere. Also what is consciousness; the awareness; the energy; the urge; that allows the mind to control the body?

And from Sir James Jeans, FRS.,

'The universe begins to look more like a great thought than like a great machine. Mind no longer appears as an accidental intruder into the realm of matter; we are beginning to suspect that we ought rather to hail it as the creator and governor of the realm of matter.'

(P137. 'The Mysterious Universe.' Cambridge University Press. 1930.)

The body we inhabit at this moment, and the world in which we live, are the result of countless lucky breaks. According to an impression that I myself received and more recently from Brigitte Rix's book, far from thought being the product of the brain it is the power of thought that gives us life. In the case of the physical universe it is the *'unified thought power'* or *'the spark of life'* a *'thought-out process'* ... *'first worked out mentally'* tried and tested in every detail by myriads of individual minds.

(P73 'Worlds Beyond the Spirit World. Brigitte Rix 'Con-Psy 2015.)

That is so hard to imagine but what I do know is that when the conditions are right *'Spirit'* <u>can</u> manipulate matter in a most amazing way. Though some physicists have linked the mind with physical events the idea that thought is the instrument of creation is the hardest proposition to swallow but mind boggling ideas are very much in tune with some present theories about the Universe. In terms of its size and the complexity of everything, does time and distance only exist whilst we are a part of it all? For instance it is said that in the spirit worlds the mind can instantly travel to places which would take light years to reach? Countless spirit minds are said to have evolved this fabulous virtual reality in which we exist which is to say the least hard to imagine and yet the levitation of heavy oak tables, furniture and even people in séances and poltergeist activity is well known. Also apports are items which are dematerialised, taken from one area and brought to another sometimes as a part of poltergeist activity or during a séance. *'White Hawk'*, controlling medium Kathleen Barkel, could cause a solid object to materialise in Maurice Barbanell's clasped hands. Beginning with a sensation of heat between the palms of his hands he gradually felt the object become solid then gradually cooling as he resumed his seat. When asked how this was accomplished White Hawk replied, *"I can only explain it by telling you that I speed up the atomic vibrations until the stones are disintegrated. Then they are brought here and I slow down the vibrations until they become solid again."* He said that the objects, which included *'semi precious stones... a sapphire set in silver, a jade ear-piece set in nine-carat gold, a gold locket and a gold ring with three opals and four diamonds,'* were not stolen but lost or buried for years or centuries, the owners having died.

(P141/2. 'This is Spiritualism.' Maurice Barbanell. Spiritualist Press. 1959)

At a John Lovette séance a young guest called Harold was warned not to touch the medium while in trance however he tried to grab a small white spirit light which floated round the room. Then a little girl's voice was heard to say:
"We are going to bring some flowers for Harold,"
'Harold groaned and said, *"This is very heavy."*
'When the lights were turned on, there was Harold with an enormous flowerpot on his lap. It was 2ft wide, one of several down in the patio. Filled with earth it weighed 200lbs and took three men to carry it back down the three flights of stairs. Unfortunately the flowers died soon after but it made a believer out of Harold.* ('Psychic News.' Feb. 19. 1977.)

The following cases involved two very startled mediums.
After a physical séance the sitters were instructed to leave the room whilst medium Alec Harris was still in the cabinet recovering. His wife Louie went downstairs to make a cup of tea when the doorbell rang. She said that she *'"could not stifle a little scream as I saw my husband, now out of*

trance, standing there, a bewildered expression on his face."' (P95. 'They Walked Among us.' by Louie Harris. Psychic Press. 1980.)

Many years ago, mediums Frank Herne and Charles Williams were holding a séance when one of the sitters jokingly suggested that the spirits try to bring Mrs Guppy, a famous medium of the time, into the séance room. Suddenly there was a heavy bump and Mrs Guppy arrived on the table holding a pen and account book. According to an anxious friend, Mrs Guppy had been sitting in her own home which was three miles away when suddenly she was gone *"leaving only a slight haze near the ceiling."*
(P133. 'Mysteries of the Afterlife.' Smyth & Stemman.
Bloomsbury Books. 42 Bloomsbury St. London. 1991.)

Then there was the Blessed Charles who levitated during contemplation and was told by the rector to come down as he was upsetting the whole community. (BBC) Perhaps the most famous case was demonstrated in the presence of several eminent men, by D.D. Home, who, in a state of trance glided through a window about seventy feet from the ground arriving feet first through the window in the next room. The windows were raised by about eighteen inches.
'Another singular phenomenon reported in connection with Home, is as bizarre as it is unaccountable, is the enormous elongation of his body, which sometimes occurred when he was in a trance. The numerous witnesses to this took every precaution to prevent themselves from being deceived.'
(P70. 'On the Threshold of the Unseen.' Sir William F Barrett. FRS. Kegan Paul. 1920.)

Crookes saw Home levitate three times whilst sitting, kneeling and standing always in good light. He also witnessed a lady levitate whilst kneeling on a chair and also two children with their chairs.
(P99 Researches into Spiritualism. Psychic Book Club 1953.)

All of this is a long way from imagining the creation of the universe. Miracles they may appear to be however if there's one thing we know for certain about our universe is that everything works in a logical fashion but! strange things do happen which seem to conform to laws that we

Page 113

have not yet discovered. What is more important to our debate is, can mankind ever have any kind of relationship with what is beyond his own three dimensional world of illusion. It appears to me that the Tibetan Buddhists might have knowledge about the mechanics of the universe, and its relationship to the mind of man, which is far in advance of Western scientific thought: What, for instance, do we make of the following idea?

'When a flag blows in the wind it is the mind that moves!'
(P253. 'With Mystics & Magicians in Tibet.' Alexandra David-Neel. Penguin. 1931.)

It is often claimed that consciousness permeates everything that is physical including rocks and plants which sounds like a very primitive idea. It makes me think of a holographic picture where each little part contains the whole. Awareness and the ability to reason would depend on the mechanisms of the body in question I would assume that smaller creatures live in the moment without the brain power to self analyse.

The question of how matter gives rise to felt experience is one of the most vexing problems we know of.....But as mathematicians work to hone and extend their tools for peering deep inside ourselves, they are confronting some eye-popping conclusions. .... suggest(ing) that ... we may have to ditch our intuitions and accept that all kinds of inanimate matter could be conscious – maybe even the universe as a whole. "This could be the beginning of a scientific revolution," says <u>Johannes Kleiner,</u> a mathematician at the Munich Centre for Mathematical Philosophy in Germany. (New Scientist May 2020.)

During her out of body experiences Rosalind A. McKnight was told, "*...Every cell in the body is a pattern of the whole, and is a universe in and of itself. All knowledge exists therein.'*
(P58 'Cosmic Journeys.' Rosalind A. McKnight. Hampton Roads. 1999.)

SURVIVAL – THE EVIDENCE
Res ipsa loquitur - The thing speaks for itself.

In 1882 the Society for Psychical Research was formed with a membership list that read more like a copy of 'Who's Who' and included some of the most eminent scientists and thinkers in the world. The SPR studied all kinds of phenomena including a huge survey of death-bed apparitions experienced at the time of death and at a distance when news of a death often took weeks to arrive. They investigated the work of mediums including physical and mental phenomena also satisfying themselves that telepathy was a fact and caused hypnosis to be more readily accepted by the BMA. One of the founders of the SPR, F.W.H Myers, a Greek scholar and fellow of Trinity College Cambridge, has continued to contribute evidence for some 30 years after his passing, the record of which is contained in the very complicated and impressive Cross-Correspondences. These were intertwining scholarly Greek texts that had meaning when fitted together which were communicated through several unconnected automatic writing mediums in different parts of the world. They ended with the request that they were to be sent to the SPR in London and signed 'FWH Myers.' More subjective material concerning the after-death state which I will return to later came through automatic writer Geraldine Cummins.
In 1858 Charles Darwin received a paper from Alfred Russell Wallace that was so like his own theory of evolution he was forced to publish. In retirement Dr., Wallace dedicated himself to the exposure of mediums because he felt they were all fraudulent parasites. He became a member of the SPR and his investigations convinced him that life after death was a fact. His book 'Miracles and Modern Spiritualism,' contrasted the attitude of the church to 'miracles and visions' experienced by the devoted, and the same phenomena witnessed by unbelievers that the clergy claimed had originated with the devil.

The Society for Psychical Research had the highest possible reputation for care and honesty and they would reject a whole series of apparently genuine séances because of the most far-fetched possibility of fraud at one sitting, in fact people often sarcastically called them, *'The Society for the Suppression of Evidence.'* Eventually some of the most sceptical, even hostile members were satisfied that life-after-death was the only answer that fitted the facts. But they had the advantage of being able to work with very powerful mediums that could produce materialisations of the human form. The organisation has never had a corporate view and nowadays there are members that consider the survival case proven and I assume those that do not. No longer do people sit staring into the fire on long winter nights which has perhaps caused the shortage of good physical mediums that will subject themselves to tests. Mediums that have been prepared to work with researchers have discovered even *if* those present are convinced the rest of the scientific community just don't want to know. Men and women of science are just as capable of making the facts fit their pet theories as anyone else so the knowledge that top scientists came to believe in a life after death may not cut any ice with the reader. - Even so one must admit that something very extraordinary must have occurred to change the minds of these individuals, many of whom were giants in their own field and had proven their ability to use logic and deduction so successfully that they were able to alter the course of science and the world in which we live. Physicists have since researched into the very foundations of matter, the fundamental building blocks of the universe, and with their theories about looking glass worlds, and parallel universes, the idea of life existing in other dimensions doesn't seem quite so farfetched. Amongst the most prominent names in psychical research were, Sir William F. Barrett.FRS whose work led towards the entoptiscope and a new optometer (For examining the eye); Sir William Crookes FRS (President of British Association for the Advancement of Science. 1898 also President of The Royal

Society.) who discovered thallium and invented the forerunner of the television tube used until the advent of flat screens; Sir Oliver Lodge. FRS who demonstrated the transmission of radio waves in 1894, one year before Marconi; Sir J.J. Thompson FRS (President 1916-1920) discoverer of the electron and John Logie Baird, (FRSE) who was able to demonstrate that the world he saw around him could be in a sense broken down into a series of codes and then reproduced using light. I.e. He invented Television.

The logic of science has removed old fears and superstitions and given us a lot to be thankful for and whilst some scientists have a religious faith simply because of the immense complexities of life, little seems to have changed after more than a century of research. The chapters of psychic science are peppered with the names of scientific men and women yet science in general is highly sceptical about all things 'paranormal.' It is the elephant in the room; it is the subject that can only be referred to in terms of utter denial: Anyone like Sir William Crookes who was brave enough to investigate mediumship was branded eccentric even though he was the recipient of many prestigious awards.

If you could travel back in time with your tape recorder, you might be called an agent of the devil simply because the people then would not know that voices could be saved in a box and listened to later. Sceptical men of science may not attribute psychic phenomena to the devil's work but because it doesn't fit in with their view of the world, either they say it can't happen, therefore it doesn't happen, or they invent some preposterous theory which makes them sound as if they understand. The problem is that the conditions required for physical research are not easily created and one of the fundamental requirements of science is that experiments are repeatable. Whilst there is stunning physical and circumstantial evidence at one end of the scale and too much nonsense at the other, researchers are likely to encounter that vast grey area of alternative explanations that lie in between. Since those days more and more information has become available for instance with improved resuscitation techniques and the advance in scanning and recording technology. As it has always been possible to create fake photographs genuine images are only really evidence for those who have taken them. The tests using computer images demonstrate that we are aware of the future, Scans show telepathic connections between individuals and the knowledge that we can be aware of being watched even through hidden cameras, has certainly strengthened the case that our capabilities extend far beyond the cranium. In terms of things that go bump in the night it is always wise to refer to 'Occam's razor' in other words looking for normal causes for unexplained lights smells or sounds before jumping to conclusions: As medium Stan Jones used to say check that the apparition that has appeared during the night isn't the newly ironed shirt hanging on the back of the door. The public face of mediums has all too often been, I'm afraid, one of odd, gullible people doing strange and ridiculous things. (With some outstanding exceptions.) It must be said that some mediums can be their own worst enemy and don't appreciate how difficult it is to defend such a complicated subject with one or two sound bites. Many TV programme makers just can't resist cutting out the most evidential bits in favour of the more bizarre sequences though in recent years some have been much more open minded. I myself am not a fan of programmes looking for ghosts because I imagine it is too easy for some wag of a camera man to produce off stage sounds.

One well-known source of evidence is concerned with bereavement and such things as chairs or objects being moved or being finely balanced one upon another also as in the song 'My Grandfather's Clock' which stopped ticking at the moment of his death. This is often put down to wishful thinking or poor observation. At least one customer thought that her deceased granddad was changing the channels on the TV, sadly it was a well known fault but there are many, many convincing accounts that the recently departed can leave a calling card. Spirit raps for instance get louder; normal raps die away whilst creaks in the fabric of the house don't respond to questioning. We have the common experience of seeing loved ones; hearing voices that help and advise; familiar smells like his pipe tobacco or her favourite perfume; mam felt dad's weight on the bed beside her. All this is explained away as the habits of a lifetime, hallucinations or the product of a disturbed mind. I do however think that certain mental illnesses might allow greater access through the unconscious which seems to be the doorway between this world and the next: Meditation or hypnosis or drugs could revive disturbing thoughts and memories which had been buried but also make the sufferer open to intrusion from equally disturbed earth-bound spirits. (Sounds like very primitive thinking I know)

I am not a medium and yet I am lucky to have seen objects controlled by some invisible power; I have had incoming thoughts; sounds; feelings; seen spirit lights and pictures and received evidential messages from people who did not know me. Though there are all kinds of research going on in many laboratories including some universities there are countless gifted individuals who are not in any kind of group but if you want knowledge or evidence a Spiritualist Church might be the easiest place to look for it. Being more concerned with evidence and philosophy it attracts the bereaved, those looking for some signs that their loved ones live on and comfort and reassurance that all will be well: Whilst it eventually became a recognised religion it is about as secular as a religion could be. The two or three hymns and opening and closing prayers are to align the mind with a higher strain of thought and provide protection. It certainly doesn't tell you what to think and not everyone is convinced but if you are religious you don't have to leave your preferred faith it can only make your belief more real. Some groups prefer a non-religious title such as 'Evidence society.' Evidence is and always has been the prime aim of Spiritualism which in its turn will hopefully make us better human beings. It is not faith based or a cult or riddled with fraud as the sceptics suggest its primary problem is the poor or variable standard of some of the mediums who demonstrate in public: Like any natural ability the very best are in the minority and I am lucky in that I have had the company of gifted friends. This has given me lots of time in which to both receive and assess the process of mediumship; always an experiment as anything communicated through the mind is bound to vary in accuracy. Even those giving and receiving messages commonly make assumptions about what they are told that is why I have always recorded my experiences which has at times highlighted mistakes and shed light on things and people I couldn't place. Such a subject is bound to attract the over imaginative some of whom believe that every word they utter is from very wise exotic guide though sometimes their open personality means that they can also get it right.

For those who claim to be aware of the so-called dead it is a privilege, an opportunity to help others to look at life from a very different angle. Only evidence can assure them and those around them that they are sensing a different reality and are not just victims of a disturbed mind or their own imagination because the two states blend and not all can recognise the difference. Some decide to be working mediums, generally unpaid often not trained in how to deliver information without adding or subtracting vital information. To avoid being influenced by the person receiving the message some insist on only 'yes,' 'no' or 'not sure' also some won't predict and concentrate only on evidence. As the mind is not constant like a radio the bad can have good days and the good can have bad days. I have known a fair few of these people, they happened to be primarily women. Occasionally a very sceptical husband would sit in the car during demonstrations until the winter time when it was very cold. Reluctantly he would come in and sit at the back of the hall then over time had to admit that his wife had very genuine abilities. The question of payment is controversial; some mediums believe they have a gift which should be shared freely however there is the question of paying the bills: Many mediums who work for the churches take only expenses for transport. Now and again special services ask for two or three pounds at the door. Mediums who work in theatres charge much more but everyone expects a message for their money which is not possible as it could take all night. I am not psychic though I have recorded 50 years of experiences and have had plenty of time to observe and assess both myself and others. Whilst some are born mediums others try to develop their sensitivity after the death of a child for example and some are brilliant though there are too many who are just not very good. When I sit with friends we always treat it as an experiment and are always wary that an odd word might have been picked up from the radio or TV though intuition is usually a good guide: Sometimes genuine information isn't confirmed for quite a time or only a few hours later.

Since 1972 I have spoken to many people mostly in their own homes and quite a few told me what they had seen, felt or heard and though I have taken them at face value, I am well aware of how unreliable memory is. When it comes to reporting a fault on their television sets most individuals are poor observers, they make things fit and embellish their stories even by telling outright fibs to sound more convincing. This did not seem to be so when it came to the more serious issues, perhaps because of the huge impact the particular incident had had on their minds. What they thought was a unique event I recognised as fitting into a known pattern and in the case of the bereaved it was something that was happening to them at the time, something they couldn't, or wouldn't talk about, even to people who were close to them. Most were more believable because they knew nothing about the subject or had been to a medium only once and casually told me about their own outstanding evidence. Like me, many were inclined to believe what they themselves had experienced but found that back in the real world it all seemed just a little too far-fetched: This of course was when few people knew anything about this subject. We see so many magicians on Television performing the impossible anyone could be forgiven for doubting what we see with our own eyes. Tremendous damage was done by Houdini who in public denounced mediums whilst privately admitting that Spiritualism was true though he was scathing about the low standards. Some experimenters have included friendly magicians as scrutineers but by no means all. I can only tell you that this phenomenon has been produced in the presence of and by ordinary men and women and that includes my friends. Reports that debunk this whole subject are quite depressing as I have had 50 years to research this stuff all of it recorded. I used to scoff myself and so had some sympathy with the sceptics however looking purely at life as we know it I tend to think that the willingness of 'intelligent' people to accept life as a happy accident is based in arrogance or fear: Of course that doesn't mean that we have to grab at any old alternative. One of the effects that I am very familiar with is the 'power' the energy present during any mediumistic endeavour. We have all felt the uplift in a crowd where there is camaraderie likewise the gloom felt in a depressing place: These effects are commonly felt by people entering someone's home. Anyone engaged in researching this subject can all but kill effects if they have the wrong attitude. Enquiring or disbelieving is fine but antagonism can change the whole atmosphere. When the power is high one can feel it in the solar plexus to the extent of sickliness but it means that mediums can work much better and physical phenomena is more likely to occur. During a physical séance the temperature can go from stiflingly hot to fridge cold in an instant so blankets may be at the ready: Distinctive cold spots can be felt in ordinary clairvoyant circles too. There are however things that I can't pick up: I am always fascinated by the subtle energies that sensitive's can feel and how informative they are about people; their ailments; attitudes; history and much more besides.

And so back to *'Shirley'* who felt that her husband had not fulfilled his promise to contact her when the time would inevitably come that they were parted. I couldn't understand this in view of what she told me.

One morning, lorry driver *'Ron'* was on his way to Yorkshire from Teesside and rang his wife *'Shirley'* at about 10:15, to see if she had received a message he was expecting. Both of them were so close that when *'Shirley'* began to feel sick shortly after, she knew something was wrong. *'Ron'* had often joked that he always drove his lorry in the fast lane and she was even more uneasy when he rang again. She asked him where he was phoning from and there was a period of silence. She couldn't hear the buzz of the car phone and asked him if he was in a phone box.

"I don't know," replied *'Ron,'* "But it's very bright and hot and I love you." after that his voice faded away. This vagueness was very unlike him as he had driven through many different countries. Later came the devastating news that he had been crushed to death by a vehicle that had crossed the central reservation, *Ron* had been in the slow lane for once! In the afternoon the policeman, who was taking *Shirley's* statement, asked about the phone call and at what time *Ron* rang. When she told him that it was several minutes after eleven he stopped writing. Another officer told her that she must have been mistaken about the time as the accident had occurred at 10:20. They had removed his legs to get him out of the lorry and he died in hospital at 11:17, shortly after the second phone call. *Shirley's* fifteen-year-old daughter had been present during the call and was able to verify the time. *Shirley* told me that because of their closeness they had made a pact that if there was any way back, who ever went first, would find it. (The names have been changed to protect privacy.)

And so amongst the myriad of opinions of over imaginative and prejudice people there is real substantial evidence verified by highly qualified scientists and witnesses that life on earth is but one tiny paragraph in the book of existence.

There are many ways in which mediums have been used to bridge the dimension gap mostly associated with giving messages and this activity has been the subject of countless studies.

Professor Archie Roy, Emeritus Professor of Astronomy at Glasgow University and former President of the Society for Psychical Research, is quoted as saying that, *'The scientific proof is so clear that only the ignorant, the intellectually arrogant, or those hide-bound in prejudice could doubt it.'*
(Cris Johnson. SPR. 'Psychic News.' July 20th 1996.)

In 2002 Professor Gary Schwartz of The University of Arizona, previously of Harvard and Yale, published 'The Afterlife Experiments,' which tested four mediums including television's John Edwards. Overseen by a committee of friendly sceptics including magicians, messages were given through intermediaries so that no audible clues could be given and were compared with placebo readings. - They were then marked for accuracy. One of the names given 'Talia' was extremely rare, the messages were lively, topical and factual giving every impression that the communicators were alive and kicking.
('The Afterlife Experiments.' Gary E. Schwartz. Atria Books 2002)

Of course this is no surprise to me after so many years of listening to mediums. I regret to say that too many are mediocre at best but can on occasion be outstanding however anything that comes through the human mind has to deal with the brain that wants to add its two penny worth. A medium has to learn how to differentiate between their own psychic impressions, thoughts from their own mind and thoughts from spirit and it's easier with some than others. A clairsentient medium can describe clothes that the communicator is wearing not by looking at an image but feeling it, if it's a tramp they can smell him also. Those who can only work with feelings or by seeing pictures are not going to be able to give names and addresses therefore it is not always easy to get the whole picture in order to avoid misunderstanding though often these mediums will receive loud thoughts or even a flash of clairaudience. The vocabulary, the personality and the ability of a medium to describe what he/she is getting will obviously have a tremendous effect upon the accuracy of the message and has as much to do with the development of new mediums as the actual act of tuning in.

The Scottish SPR tested the theory that all communications are so general that they could apply to anyone: This proved not to be true. The Scottish Medium, Barber, Gordon Smith was one of the highest achievers producing highly relevant and personal material. Gordon had taken part in double blind tests and in some cases the sitter didn't know that they were getting a sitting until afterwards.

('The Heaven & Earth Show.' BBC1 Television. 25.6.2000.)

Sir Oliver Lodge once asked his wife and 11 children to pretend that he was speaking to them from beyond the grave. He told them to ask questions about things they had shared together which would prove who he was. He couldn't even remember one of them. *"I am obviously not your father,"* he told them. ('Psychic News.' Sept 7th 1996.)

Working with symbols can cause problems when they are misinterpreted. One medium saw a broken ring and wrongly assumed that it referred to a broken marriage. It turned out to be a ring that was so tight it had to be cut off. I was once told by a medium that I knew a sea-faring man. When I said I didn't think so she decided that I might be the sailor. After several attempts to get the sailor to fit in somewhere she said in exasperation. 'Well why are they showing me a parrot in a cage?' to which I replied, "Because one bit me last week." I have had incredibly accurate messages from total strangers. Since the beginning of my adventures my recordings have provided useful information when people that I didn't recognise were eventually identified. I had been given the name Eddie many times and then a medium described a sailor drowning at Scapa flow. There were a lot of facts and names in the message but I couldn't could place any of it. However an aunt went through it all, and explained who the people were with the exception of Eddie. Some weeks later my brother in law told me that Eddie was his brother and was drowned at Scapa flow. Was this the seafaring man? This illustrates the need for detail in communications to avoid assumptions. Anyone new to this subject will think, fraud, magic, gullible: In physical séances demonstrating that events are genuine is very much a part of the procedure with mediums being, searched, tied up with plastic straps etc. The Afterlife Experiments used magicians to oversee the mediums however with those who receive messages from mediums there can be a lot of assumptions made. I have done it myself but was able to discover the real truth because of my recordings. We often go to a medium with a certain person uppermost in the mind also there may be messages from someone we have long forgotten. Whilst trying to help the sitter to understand the message the medium may change the sense of it without realising it: Sometimes what has been given may be a metaphor not meant to be taken literally. I find the most unusual or bizarre messages are the most evidential and often quite simple. Deciphering messages sometimes needs a lot of experience as the message sender or senders try to cram as much information into one short session as possible. While you are wondering how Uncle Tommy, who was small, fat and bald, is being described as a tall grey haired man they may actually be two different people or someone else in the room might say, 'I think you're with me.' A good medium will do his or her best to clarify the message but in the short time available, mistakes can be made hence the advisability of note taking. Some mediums see a light above the correct person or even a figure standing behind the sitter. A simple word or mannerism can have a tremendous impact and be as emotional, and evidential, as a name and address. It is the unusual things that are most striking; a message from Harry number one to Harry number two included broken pipes and the name Jack; Harry number two used to smoke broken pipes and he was so small they used to call him Jack-in-the-box. One lady was given a memory of holding the mercury, from a broken barometer, in her hand and when a medium described a man holding a rabbit by the back legs she was alarmed when the recipient said that it was a cat. It turned out that the cat was alive and the man always carried it that way. One medium described a green horse, it turned out to be a doorstop that had been thrown at the sitter's husband. The same lady was reminded of the time that she played hoopla with a ring of black pudding. Names are less common though I was given my Dad's full name by two different people, both complete strangers; one became my good friend Ian Veril, born with mediumistic abilities that sometimes frightened his wife when things moved around in the house: He was later to become leader of our circle. We never got what we were sitting for i.e. the trumpets whizzing around producing voices from the other side but what happened was totally unexpected. Recently I was relating the following to my son who remember told me,

"If you weren't my dad I would say you were stark raving mad."

When I was an apprentice Television Engineer I used to assemble Seymour floating television tables - Never in my wildest dreams did I imagine that one would actually float in mid-air at our small, weekly physical circle. Luminous tags were attached and we could feel it especially when it landed on someone's lap where it stayed rock solid until asked to move. We asked spirit to move some wind chimes contained in an open box whereupon the table tipped up and appeared to direct energy towards them with very noisy results. We could often hear the raps of invisible fingers and once actually recognised that they belonged to a lady, a man and a child. In spite of all my years of research the reality of this situation was very striking. Apart from the table and plastic garden chairs the only other thing in the small dining room was a music centre including a dvd player. This was switched at the beginning of every sitting with the sound of Meatloaf's *'No matter what'* blasting out until it was switched off again by invisible hands.

When Ian saw a particular gent wearing a top hat and carrying an old fashioned case sitting on the end of his bed which was depressed with his weight, he knew it mean bad news: This was to be the illness from which he eventually died. Ian's son was on Skype one day when his friend asked him who the old man with the top hat and case was standing beside him. As Ian was telling how his Doctor friend often moved things around there was a loud clatter as if to confirm that he was listening. He was obviously a family member from the past as he looked very similar to Ian's son and his relative Stephen King. Ian passed over on August 6th 2007.

Some of the so called dead obviously take any opportunity to let their loved ones know that they are still around. My friend Allan Bowes who died in 2005, was seen by his wife Val large as life walking from the other end of the caravan and sitting down on the couch. My mother-in-law, a strong catholic, was beginning to have her doubts until she saw my father-in-law skip across the bedroom in a 'flowers that bloom in the spring tra la, la,' kind of way and glowing with happiness. She said, "He looked so real that I could have reached out and touched him."

Clinical Psychologist Dr. Tanya Byron told colleague Prof Richard Bentall that she had seen her father sitting in her hotel room shortly after he had died. Prof Bentall said that these kinds of *'hallucinations'* were very common amongst the bereaved. ('Am I normal', BBC2 TV 2008.)

It seems that some Psychologists have never considered that some of the so-called hallucinations might be real individuals just as the SPR survey had found.

Those who die instantaneously due to an explosion perhaps or a gunshot might believe that they are still alive and well, a very confusing situation as suddenly they are invisible to those around them who are still living and there are some graphic descriptions of this. To be told that they are now dead is understandably not always believed. Robert Monroe described a scene in 42nd Street New York. A *'bewildered '* man trying to flag down a taxi, a long- haired youth trying to gain the attention of a group of youngsters smoking a joint and *'The burly policeman in full uniform swinging his night stick, strolling along the store fronts totally unaware that he is unobserved. The smartly dressed woman ...'* *opening her purse'*... as she unknowingly walks through the side of a nearby building.

('Far Journeys.' P194. Robert Monroe. Doubleday. 1985.)

Mary Ann Winkowski has seen ghosts ever since she was two years old. She hears and speaks to them mentally which is useful when she is told something that the other people in the room would be better off not hearing as the ghost has been able to see everything that is going on in the house! As a child she would see ghosts at funerals watching events then her Italian grandma from whom she inherited her psychic abilities (though not the ability to see Ghosts.) would say, *"Tell them they should leave now."* Always there was a *'white light...hovering nearby'* into which they would walk then fade away. (P20.) She says that many ghosts are frightened of the light, sometimes with good reason, but others are very religious and *'fear the judgement they might face.'* (P92.) Once spirits move to this higher level Mary, Ann can no longer communicate with them though she has medium friends who can. She writes that there are no earth-bound spirits with them when they are working though they can be present when people are using an Ouija board and be somewhat of a nuisance if they are intent upon telling lies. She says there are likely to be much fewer ghosts at a cemetery than a theatre, where there are lots of people. (P165.) On one occasion the murder victim pointed out the murderer who was tried and convicted of the crime.

('When Ghosts Speak.' Mary, Ann Winkowski. Hodder/Mobious. 2008.)

Amongst the countless reports of ghosts there is compelling evidence that they have been mistaken for real people whose identity was later confirmed. Though messages can be a very powerful indicator that our relatives are still around, seeing and hearing are still thought of as being the ultimate in proof. Leslie Flint couldn't enjoy a film because of the voices that would annoy other patrons in the cinema. In his séances famous people including 'Dame Ellen Terry,' 'Oscar Wilde', 'Rupert Brooke,' 'Mahatma Gandhi' and 'Cosmo Gordon Lang', the former Archbishop of Canterbury, used to speak, their recognisable voices coming from mid air. Leslie, the most tested medium around, was unusual in that he did not have to provide any equipment: He was tested with his mouth filled with water then taped up and yet the voices were still heard.

('Life After Death.' Neville Randall. Corgi. 1975.)

Archbishop Lang, commissioned a report on Spiritualism which turned out to be favourable and then kept it secret. Later it was leaked to the Psychic News. Lang spoke through the mediumship of Leslie Flint using the independent direct voice:

"Where Spiritualism is concerned ... I was afraid it could undermine the Church and probably even destroy it, and I was not sure that it had very much to offer that was good. 'Of course many of those ideas I have now changed. I do feel very strongly that it is a thing that is so vital and so important that all peoples should be conscious and know about it.... I do feel,"' he added, "' that it is dangerous if it is used in the wrong sense. 'If you go on to contact the highest forms, the good forces, those who can help the world, those who can uplift mankind, you must have instruments who are of like mind and like thought and it seems to me that many of these instruments are of a very, unfortunately, low order ... lower entities who are earthbound ... can ...speak to people and tell them things which are not true. I realise that out of this which you term Spiritualism there is much good to come. In fact it is obviously the essence of the early church.

(P160. 'Life After death.' Neville Randall. Corgi. 1975.)

Most of these kinds of séances use small aluminium cones with luminous tabs. At one end you can hear faint twittering, (Lip smacking) the sound of an un-amplified voice whilst at the other, a relative speaking to someone in the audience like Marie McGlynn, who at a Colin Fry séance on, June 17th 1988, laughed and joked with her husband Nick, a few hours after she had died.

At a private séance with Stewart Alexander we saw trumpets flying about at tremendous speed, at one moment rapping on the ceiling then in a split second from somewhere else in the room. And if you think such a profound subject is demeaned by such party tricks it is merely a demonstration of power, rather like the prisoner who raps on the pipes to assure his fellow prisoners in the adjacent cells that they are not alone. Stewart was tied to the chair with cable ties which were removed by dematerialising them then re-materialising after being replaced on his wrists. On one occasion this happened too early which burned his wrist.

We saw a small hand materialise which was grasped by a couple from Switzerland, this was a young female relative. Whilst the hand was obviously solid it looked snowy like the picture on an old TV would be on a slightly weak signal. Seeing is believing, or so they say. The ultimate proof of survival would be to speak to someone you know to be dead, even then you might convince yourself that this had been a hallucination you would require further proof that the experience had not been the product of an overheated imagination brought about perhaps by grief. The suggestion that the dead can return is so sensational, so unbelievable it surely proves that all Spiritualists are as mad as hatters. It's all very well to theorize, to sit in judgment, but when it happens to you, nothing on earth will overturn your conviction that what you have seen is real. By all the tests of observation, witness, common sense and technology, materialisations *are* real but only those that have seen for themselves know that. Unfortunately there isn't space to include the many details which surround the following sketches but I hope that what follows will have the ring of truth about it.

In 1870 Mr William Crookes FRS (Later Sir William Crookes president of the Royal Society.) was pressurised by fellow scientists into investigating the phenomena called Spiritualism because they were sure that he would expose it as a complete fraud. In the presence of the great medium D.D. Home he saw an accordion playing inside a cage and measured an unknown force on a plank of wood, all documented as with any scientific experiment. But his colleagues suddenly didn't want to know and wouldn't become involved. These experiments lead Crookes to work with a young medium called Florence Cook and to come face to face with a materialised spirit, 'Katie King', the daughter of the famed buccaneer John King. In 1874 the young medium Florence Cook held séances in Crookes' laboratory and her parent's house in Hackney at which Katie King materialised. Katie often cut parts off her dress and presented them to sitters then with a wave of her hand the holes disappeared and the pieces of material mostly melted into thin-air. All manner of tests were made including the taking of photographs but the ultimate proof to those present that this was not some clever actress smuggled into the séance room was Katie's dematerialisation described by medium Florence Marryat in her book "There is No Death." (Sir Arthur Conan Doyle gave Miss Marryat a glowing reference.) She said that the first time she met Florence Cook was when her little daughter appeared through her.) (P135.)

'...all present decided we would prefer to witness the effect of a full glare of gas upon the materialised form than to have the usual sitting, as it would settle the vexed question of the necessity of gloom (if not darkness) for a materialising séance forever. We accordingly told 'Katie' of our choice, and she consented to stand the test though she said afterwards we had put her to much pain. She took up her station against the drawing-room wall with her arms* *extended as if she were crucified. Then three gas-burners were turned on to their full extent, in a room about sixteen feet square. The effect upon 'Katie King' was marvellous. She looked like herself for the space of a second only, then she began to gradually melt away. I can compare the dematerialization of her form to nothing but a wax doll melting before a hot fire. First the features became blurred and indistinct; they seemed to run into each other. The eyes sunk in the sockets, the nose disappeared, the full frontal bone fell in. Next the limbs appeared to give way under her, and she sank lower and lower on the carpet like a crumbling edifice. At last there was nothing but her head left above the ground; then a heap of white drapery only, which disappeared with a whisk, as if a hand had pulled it after her, and we were left staring by the light of three gas-burners, at the spot on which 'Katie King' had stood.'*

(P139. 'Researches in the Phenomena of Spiritualism.'
William Crookes, FRS. 1870. Psychic Book Club. 1953.)

In order that the spirit body can become more solid, and therefore visible, it must attract physical matter with which to clothe itself. Ectoplasm, a mucus-like substance, is drawn from the orifices of mediums and sitters and has at times the appearance of butter muslin, so much so that sceptics have accused mediums in the past of concealing the material about their person. In materialising séances the medium is often placed in a cabinet, usually formed by a curtain across the corner of the room, in order that the ectoplasm can be gathered in one place by spirit operators. I'm told that something must be drawn from material in the room because the curtains and carpets show signs of a marked deterioration where the same place has been used for a long time. It is hard to imagine any method that might be employed to duplicate the following reports as the ectoplasmic material appears to have a life of its own. It can swirl about like a white mist and has what Michael Bentine describes as *'A distinctive smell like that of ozone'.*

('The Door Marked Summer'. P292.Michael Bentine. Granada 1981.)

Page 133

Friends tell me that it can feel clammy. Professor Arthur Ellison described it as being like *"solidified cold porridge.'*

('The Reality of the Paranormal.' P55. Professor Arthur Ellison. Harrap 1988.)

Because ectoplasm usually dissolves when exposed to light, the best results are obtained in complete darkness: This somewhat defeats the object of convincing the sceptic except in terms of the voices and the touch of the spirit people. Many materialisations are illuminated only by luminous plaques, or lights that the spirits bring with them. Though white light has been used on rare occasions the modern favourite is a red pigmy lamp after the manner of the photographic darkroom. Ectoplasm has its own luminosity and does not reflect the red light. John Reimer often shook materialised hands and found that the distinctive smell, and the luminosity, remained on his hand. Physical effects have been produced in good white light but this depends upon the amount, and the type of power available from the medium who is usually in trance, at least part of the time. - There are however some who remain conscious throughout the proceedings. The tremendously sudden drop in temperature can be an indication of genuine physical phenomena which I myself have experienced though at many séances everyone gets very, very warm. It can take years to create the right conditions for spirit return but they can in fact occur spontaneously, when for example ghosts or apparitions are seen. Ghosts have been reported being able to lift heavy objects and even eat a meal - and in full daylight too! And so we return to the wife of our first witness, Sir William Crookes. During a séance in a London house with D.D.Home, Lady Crookes described what she saw: -

"Home was holding an accordion which 'was immediately taken from his hand by a cloudy appearance which soon seemed to condense into a distinct human form, clothed in a filmy drapery...The accordion began to play...and the figure advanced toward me till it almost touched me... It was semi-transparent, and I could see the sitters through it all the

time. Mr Home remained near the sliding doors. As the figure approached I felt an intense cold, getting stronger as it got nearer, and as it was giving me the accordion I could not help screaming. The figure immediately seemed to sink into the floor to the waist, leaving only the head and shoulders visible, still playing the accordion, which was then about a foot off the floor. Mr Sergeant Cox was rather angry at my want of nerve, and exclaimed: "Mrs. Crookes, you have spoilt the finest manifestation we have ever had."'
(P238. 'Mysteries of the Afterlife.' Smyth & Stemman. Bloomsbury Books. 1991.)

Tom Harrison's Aunt Agg materialised week after week six years after her 'death' and was photographed at their home circle in Middlesbrough. - Tom, a down- to-earth, no-nonsense, individual told us that he had spoken to, shaken hands with, or embraced, some 1,500 materialised spirit people! Tom passed in 2010 and materialised at the Felix circle in Germany in 2012 in bright light.
(Visits by our Friends from the Other Side by Tom Harrison. VHS Video.)

Desmond Leslie described an Alec Harris séance in a Cardiff semi:-

'The sitters were crammed into the small bedroom watching a procession of individuals of different nationalities, swathed in 'towels', come from behind the curtain which served as a makeshift cabinet in the corner of the room and was barely big enough for Harris' chair. Each one looked around the room calling out the names of the people they recognised. On several occasions one of them remained over-long and began to collapse like an inflatable doll with a leak, before struggling back to the cabinet. It was not until I saw the face of one collapse and run away like melted ice cream that I could fully assure myself that I was really seeing "ghosts" and not a parade of Harris' actor friends suitably dressed for the occasion .... 'It was the very ordinariness, homeliness and good humour of the materialised beings that made it hard to believe that they were not real in the sense that we are. But then, if they were the ectoplasmic-swathed spirits of

ordinary people, how else should they behave other than as ordinary people? I became acutely aware of the smell (which was) not unlike the smell of hydrochloric acid.'

'The scientist... asked me to take hold of his hand. I plucked up courage and grasped a perfectly firm human hand, normal in every respect except one ...(it) felt rather like a piece of furniture. I asked him what it felt like to do this. "Not very nice my friend. It's rather like diving into a tank of black oil."... you have no idea how heavy are your physical bodies...when you come back to the physical scene direct from the freedom and lightness of the astral world, it is quite a nasty shock when you feel the weight again.

(Psychic News. 'What a Way to Run a Universe.' Desmond Leslie.)

Whilst in trance a medium can look something like the person who is speaking through him or her. Apparently, in some cases, the face can change dramatically, though quite slowly, as if it was made of rubber. With transfiguration there is a mask built up out of ectoplasm that attempts to reflect the face of the communicator: The effect is incredibly impressive, one second we see the face of the medium in clear red light, the next we see a completely different face. Everyone, whether clairvoyant or not, will be able to see a transfiguration because it is physical. Often someone will come through a sitter and will only be seen by the clairvoyants. This is probably why some people claim that a particular medium was brilliant whilst others put it down to 'face pulling.' I was present when Stan Jones held a transfiguration service at a packed Redcar Church: Illuminated by a light just in front of him his face became that of his guide *'White Wing'* a typical American Indian Chief with head dress; a much longer face; larger nose, pouched cheeks and bare chest this image glowed with light. Later Churchill appeared and talked about the future, sadly I didn't record it as it seemed pretty generalised. Only when his prediction came true did I realised that it was about the coming austerity.

Michael Bentine described a sitting by a Mrs Balmer in the drawing room in ordinary light. *'Her whole head now appeared to be covered by a fine misty veil, which somehow seemed to be endowed with a form of life and movement of its own. This formed into features which suddenly sprang into abrupt focus and were clearly visible for some fifteen seconds or so. The impression given was quite startling and in no way suggested contortion of the medium's features ... somehow the whole hair style would change; hats would appear and dematerialise; and the faces ranged from those of young girls and women through boys and young men to old people of both sexes. Even clothes of a sort, such as the top of a Victorian high-necked blouse or part of a uniform would appear and then melt away; beards, moustaches and hair, changing from long lustrous coils of feminine locks to short curly hair and even complete baldness - all seemed to manifest in that strange swirling mist ... I was fascinated by the obvious excitement of the people round me as they recognised some relative or close friend.'*

('The Door Marked Summer.' P114. Michael Bentine. Granada. 1981)

Cyril Permutt found that forms including hands and faces could be photographed before being visible to the naked eye. They were in themselves slightly luminous, often transparent and sometimes only two-dimensional. These flat images can look more like cutouts from a magazine. *'There were very evident life-like movements in these images which rapidly succeeded one after another and seemed to be living things'*

(P145. Photographing the Spirit World. Cyril Permutt. Aquarian Press. 1983.)

David Sinclair describes an occasion at a Luisito seance when a single materialised hand floated towards the ceiling and a lady said in a loud voice. *"That's being done with smoke and a movie projector."* The hand paused then came streaking down towards the woman. The next thing they heard was a loud smack on the head then she howled in pain. (Pagans, Priests and Prophets. David Sinclair. Prentice Hall. U/S.1957.)

In November 1994, Frankie Brown was invited to John Austin's Home Circle with the medium "Lincoln" (((Colin Fry))) In total darkness Alan Brown materialised, walked across the room and held his mother's hand. Alan, who was murdered 14 years ago, bent down and gave her a long kiss on the cheek after which the pair had a *"long, loving, evidential chat"* thus proving that it is not always necessary to see to believe. (P12. Noah's Ark Newsletter. Jan. 1995.)

When the earth was first photographed from space it changed the outlook of millions, when the dead return it changes the outlook of a few invited guests: Such is the power of the illusion that death is the end; the evidence suggests that you cannot die for the life of you. So far I have stayed within the bounds of fact but now, whilst 'I' think the following contributions are broadly true and have the ring of truth, you may have to be content that they are simply food for thought.

GOD

The last big question is that of God but how do we picture Him? In the film "Oh God," George Burns, playing the part of God, had to resort to a few party tricks, like making it rain inside the car, and becoming invisible in the court room to convince the hero that he really was who he said he was. Mankind looks at the universe and thinks that God has left His creation perhaps to begin some new project somewhere in the vastness of space: Like a tractor given to a poor society to plough the fields to use as they wish. When a body is severely damaged without the ability to communicate we assume that the house is empty, the occupant gone away. One day that individual is presented with a word processor and the marvel of electronics shows us that inside the apparently empty shell there dwells a mind of great sensitivity and intelligence: What we have seen is not what it appeared to be. Maybe we haven't seen the obvious, that all of the intelligence which surrounds us including yours, including mine, is evidence of the existence of God. If life after death is a fact there are going to be intelligences so far advanced that we might also think of them as Gods though perhaps they wouldn't describe themselves in that way. If we are part of one great consciousness then in some sense we have our own God, the part of us which is individualised and has progressed through many, many lives but which manifests only in part through the human brain with its relatively tiny capacity. Therefore we have *the God without and the God within* and so we judge ourselves, what fairer system could there be? God is not an old man in the sky with a magic wand but an intelligent creative energy an integral part of all beings who at our level are limited by the capacity of the brain and are generally only aware of the experiences of this present lifetime. So we are overshadowed in effect by our own personal God who doesn't interfere with our free will because the world couldn't work like that, but together with the helpers influences us through our inner minds to get the best out of life - if we will listen! Eternity is filled with countless beings all at different stages progressing towards the source from which we came: (Am I any the wiser about God, the source, the *start* of it all? I haven't a clue)

...in the mind of man the voice of God is silent is never heard, no one ever has a conversation with God save that they tell Him what they want, and ask for improbable things. (Feb 2020) Even the most hardened sceptic will call on God to save him as he falls over a cliff. Mankind needs a kind of superman figure, who, at the end of the day when the chips are down, can come to the rescue. Of course he never does, at least not in the way we expect so what does that really mean in practical terms? What does 'He' know of you and me? Are we mere images in the mind of God the inventor; the creator; the parent; the teacher: Is He/She really someone to whom we can relate and go to for advice, someone who can comfort us when things go wrong? I asked about The Father and His place in the scheme of things. 'Does he take the pain away, does he actively help?' *Well on occasions we would say yes because he is the instigator and we are the chaplains, we are the activators* (Like permanent members of staff?) *Got it in one.* (2019.)

But just a minute, if God is the sum total of everything He tolerates some pretty mean and evil people. Can the suffering of an innocent child be justified in order that man might have free will? In the Jim Carey film, 'Bruce Almighty,' the Hero temporarily deputising for God, answers the multitude of prayers in his 'In box' with a click of the mouse thereby giving every individual what he or she asks for and resulting in absolute chaos. Discussing the film on BBC's 'Heaven & Earth Show,' Irma Kurtz and Anthony Wilson were asked what they would do if they were God: Both agreed that they would do nothing and that that would be the hardest thing. (BBC1. 29th June 2003.)

Rabbi Lionel Blue once asked himself why God didn't take a hand in all this then he remembered that God had no hands. Because of free will the bad that the un-progressed spirits and human beings do is done within the mind of God and therefore each one will eventually work their way back towards brighter regions under God's watchful eye; the God, within our own higher self. When the innocent suffer that is the hardest thing of all even though a child has been an adult many times. Its spirit has entered this life in the full knowledge of its future challenges and though that spirit is part of God Himself and there is precious knowledge gained at the end of it all, it is still so hard to accept.

But it's a contrast never forget that for where there is pain there is joy in the making (Jan 2020)

The onlooker in the death camp saw the three hanged: The two men were soon dead but the fifteen-year-old boy still moved, his lighter weight had kept him alive. A voice in the crowd asked, *"Where is God now?"* As they filed past him he still moved. For half an hour he lived and the man at the back said again, *"Where is God now?"* A voice within the onlooker's head said,
"There He is. Hanging on the rope."

('Evil' ITV Channel 4. Oct. 1990.)

'...God is Sovereign not in Heaven alone but in Hell also, and in all the Hells He rules and He alone. The others dominate locally, but he rules over them all ... Evil men by many are thought to be outside the pale of His Kingdom; and evils and disasters to be faulty manifestations of His dynamic energising. But both are in His hands to use, and even evil men, unwittingly are made to work out His plans and purpose in the ultimate.'

(P152. 'The Ministry of Heaven.' Rev. Vale Owen. Inspired writing. 1920.)

On holiday some years ago, my wife Ann, who is more interested in helping people in this life than worrying about an afterlife, answered a question I was quietly pondering on. She said that something had been going around in her head all day but she didn't know what it meant, she said, *"God is the sum total of the higher selves."*

Coral Polge a superb Psychic portrait artist, (She drew 'dead' people) told of an experience she found 'almost impossible to describe' ... *'I had gone back beyond everything to that minute spark within, which is a part of God; a golden spark, warm and beautiful. A state of absolute joy engulfed me.'...'That little spark is a tiny blueprint of the whole universe, and within that spark is all the knowledge of eternity, all that has ever been or will be, and in that complete silence in a fraction of time, suddenly you know that you are one with God, and that everyone and everything is God.'... 'I was aware of oceans, fine grains of sand, planets, trees, people and animals, of everything that existed, and there was no such thing as time ... God is a creative, thinking, loving Energy, and the memory of that creation is there within each one of us. We created the universe ... I could recall-if recall is the right word - being part of that moving consciousness in space, building planets, manipulating suns. Built and destroyed, they explode, implode, and we, the energy which created them, go on re-designing, re-creating from cosmic dust. But we never cease to go on learning ... We are all seeking an understanding of darkness in order to comprehend the light.'* (P64. 'Living Images.' Coral Polge & Kay Hunter. The Aquarian Press. 1985.)

The inspirers of the Reverend Stainton Moses put it like this:-
'... We present to you a Deity whose name, as revealed is Love. Love confined within no limits ... God is no person. He is enthroned in no place, but is all pervading, ever existing; guiding and loving all ... God as far as we have known Him, is not a limited personality nor was He ever enshrined in a human body, or amenable to human influence. The deity operates by general laws. ...On the one hand we have to avoid the fatal error that seeks to reduce God to a force; and on the other, to guard against the anthropomorphic delusion which pictures a humanity with man's failings and necessities and insatiable craving for power ... God is really an informing, energising Spirit.

*He supplies the light and love that give beauty to all
around you. The divine life is brought home to you in the
life of Christ. God is not a force nor the impersonal entity
you call nature. Try and regard Him as the Informing
Spirit, permeating all. The word Father is the true
conception. Nature is not God but a manifestation of the
Supreme. The hand is not the body, but it is the
manifestation of that which makes up the body.*

('*More Spirit Teachings.*' P20. Rev Stainton Moses. (Died 1892.) 1952.)

Musical analyst, '*Sir Donald Tovey*' speaking to Rosemary
Brown had this to say:-

'*There are not, as it would appear, two creative aspects,
viz. male and female, but one only, the creative energy
force which divides and sub-divides to produce numerous
forms and formation of matter ... The life - or energy force -
is single, whole, formless, soundless and more powerful
than all its combined manifestations and is the only
absolute complete life essence.*' '*All manifestations are
incomplete or partial expressions of that which can never
be fully expressed in any term other than its own; it is the
incomprehensible yet all comprehending; that which could
be called God the Fundamental, Absolute and Eternal
Being. This definition may sound formal and formidable to
those who are accustomed to cultivating the image of a
personal God; yet this same Being is involved with each
and every human being. It motivates all life, and directs its
undivided attention to every part of creation from the great
spheres of light and cauldrons of energy to the tiniest
flower unfolding its petals upon the earth.*' '*This Wondrous
Being who can count the number of hairs on a head
however lavish the locks, and who notices the fall of a
sparrow. It is the all-governing Being which in splendour,
is unimaginable, in majesty, indescribable, in all
embracing awareness, unfathomable. This, the
Unknowable is All Knowing, inaccessible but having
access to all. Its veritable essence is the energy-force which
functions perpetually to perpetuate life. It emits qualities of
perfect order, balance, harmony and health, and is*

Page 143

constant in its drive towards the repair and renewal of systems and nature where they have fallen into defect through the uncontrolled vagaries of energies it has released and to which it has allotted self-expression.' In other words mankind. He goes on to say that there is no opposing force and that 'conflict, malformation, confusion, afflictions of mind and body, and subsequent suffering,' result from the free will bestowed upon some if its creations.

('Unfinished Symphonies.' P111/112. Rosemary Brown. Pan Books. 1971.)

Creative thought power has always existed! It is the basis to everything! An 'ocean of eternal thought Power which has always existed and will exist forever. ... it never had a starting point.....it has the built in urge.. to ...expand, to multiply and to create. Energy never dies or disappears....It can only change form or intensity.

(P39/40Truths, lies and Distortions, Brigitte Rix 2012 CON-PSY Publications.)

For those who are looking for a Father figure there is the God within also the helpers even though we are generally not aware of them. They do not need to be physically present as a thought sent out is received in an instant. There is a power always with us even during the darkest moments which like the highest mountain in the world we have climbed and triumphed over as a willing participant in this amazing adventure that we call life.

God is with you in his entirety, for the absolute overall; consciousness is always one with all its constituent parts so your wish to have an overall parent, teacher, guardian is in that respect true. However the work that we do is for us; to solve the problems; to make the progress; to reach out into the higher realms; to come to terms with what is; what life offers us to accept it gratefully. To be pleased to be able to be in this world of great wonders participating in a great scheme which is the creation of mankind for the purposes of that peculiar experience which he has to offer both in creating the world but also accepting its conditions, its rules, and the joy of taking part in all the activities which present themselves. Teach yourself to smile more often, in the greater scheme of things nothing is ever that bad that it cannot be overcome. Once these things have passed through your consciousness they are no longer required. Lesson learned; job done; move on. (October 2019)

The Heaven of which you speak is with you now, round and about you, making inroads into your thinking, joining with you in impossible adventures. For the human mind knows no bounds, everything it wishes comes true if not in reality in dreams. Exploring the way out of trouble; seeing things realistically; opening doors in the mind and reaching out to other dimensions. All this it can do and more:- Sorting out your problems; giving you the agenda for the day; climbing little by little, step by step, you move nearer ever nearer to God in your search for truth and wisdom and understanding. Everything you learn is precious, everything you understand is valuable and even when you do not understand it is a marker; a pointer; a deal with destiny a recognition of something that needs to be understood; sorted; fixed and regenerated even. The God within you knows all; hears all; sees all and feels all. It is not isolated as you are but far ranging. It reaches out to other souls to blend as one; to fix problems and to keep thinking. Opportunities abound because of this network of friends, even people you don't know coming together to make it happen. Love is always around you and about you inspiring; opening doors and reaching out to other people. The way forward is clear; heaven is where the heart is. The underlying reasons for your life on earth acts as a catalyst which will bring you into certain situations to meet certain people to understand certain things. Nothing is left untouched, nothing is left not understood and all is included in this great plan that you might move forward in your own way in your own time but within these parameters that you might meet the objectives and go the mileage to reach the goal that you have set.

('The Spiritual Life.' P100 30th July 2015)

Page 145

GUIDANCE

Everything that happens in the world is the result of sheer hard work and ingenuity, work is the bread of life and as life goes on eternally so too does work. Sitting on a cloud all day playing a harp might be all right for the musically minded but there is a world to run and people to look after. Somebody knows when a sparrow dies, the hairs on your head are counted and haphazard though your life may appear to be, somebody knows, somebody cares: You have a goal to reach; a deadline to meet, the show goes on and behind it all are the backroom boys working very hard to make it all happen. Each individual is a part of one harmonious whole: Imagine a spider's web, touch it anywhere and the vibrations reach out to every part of it. We think of a person in spirit and he/she responds, we live in a sea of thought yet we are able to tune into that unique wavelength. This is the stuff of basic electronics, tuning the radio to pick up one particular station, like the Internet, we each have our own e-mail address - our personality. It would appear that unlike light which has a fixed speed thought is instant which would place it outside the known laws of the universe. Man must have free will to go his own way, to make his own mistakes and to take credit for his own successes but by the same token he must be free to help another and to ask for help. All of us have to go to school to be taught by someone older and wiser, everyone is in the position of having to pass knowledge on to someone else; to guide and to help whether at home, work or play. The need is greater when that person is in trouble and if he is to get the best from being on earth it may be necessary that he has a little prompting especially at crucial times in his life. The vast majority of mankind probably have no idea why they were born; they just get on with it and it seems only fair that someone tries to point them in the right direction. Whilst we may not have memories of a previous existence there must be something in our makeup that has learned the lessons and which sounds warning bells when we slip backwards. No one is alone there are countless individuals in and around this ball of clay helping mankind, some of whom we may have had strong connections with for centuries. They may feel that they can use their particular strengths to help you to avoid making the same mistakes as they did and perhaps to compensate for letting someone else down in their previous existence? What can be said of the good can surely be said of the less progressed for if those in the world of spirit are drawn to us out of some kind of empathy they may perhaps be a hindrance because in our darker moments their influence might envelope us and make it harder to shake off negative thoughts and gloomy feelings. Likewise in seeking inspiration the more pure our thoughts the more we come into tune with higher spirits. Could the loud thought that everyone takes for granted be the voice of spirit friends? Nobody ever marvels that his or her own mind can act like an independent intelligence, an inner voice which presents all of the arguments against what you are determined to do come hell or high water. Perhaps it's just the mind's way of presenting a rounded summary of the situation but I am satisfied that when an odd thought steals into an empty mind there just might be somebody there. I believe that the thoughts of the helpers are such an everyday occurrence that, like the sound of the birds, they often go unnoticed. It has been proved to me many times that thoughts can steal into all of our minds which did not originate in the memory. Assessing the truth of life after death caused me to think long and hard, I had never ever been aware of anything outside of the normal workaday world but like doubting Thomas I was desperate to see for myself. Suddenly it seemed to me that someone outside of me was patiently demonstrating his or her presence. What I call 'loud thoughts' would appear in my mind and they were unexpected and unusual, often they were tunes. This was my idea chosen to identify individuals because they are more noticeable than words but so what if a tune is going round and round in my head I probably picked it up off the radio. But what a coincidence, someone has walked across the workshop and turned up the TV sound for a couple of seconds. The melody which is accompanying the interval between school programmes is the one I thought of earlier but it's not the usual repetitive test card stuff that we used to start humming seconds before hand. Every morning I would be treated to a loud-thought tune and within two or three hours a complete stranger would have whistled or sung it as though it had just popped into his/her head or I would turn the car radio on and it would be there. But there was more to it, I knew the thought wasn't just any old random tune or word I had a definite knowing just the same as when you know someone has spoken to you. It was unexpected and often unusual and sometimes it was just the strength or the persistence of it. I faithfully recorded every impression and was always amazed each time it was confirmed but occasionally a word would be quite meaningless. One night, as I closed my eyes, I received the thought, 'Ichabod.' In the morning it was there again. I looked it up. 'Child of no glory.' I didn't like the sound of that. The next day I was in a rush as TV engineers frequently are, I came out of a customer's house, got into the car, turned the ignition on and with it the radio. The first word I heard was 'Ichabod' and I was so amazed at the coincidence that I sat and listened to the programme; the lady in question was talking about her childhood games. When things were nice like scrunching leaves underfoot or running your toes through the sand you called it *'through leaves.'* Anything unpleasant was called, *'unthrough leaves'* and something really irritating like a sticking drawer was called *'Ichabod.'* Now I have many failings but I could well have been christened Ichabod. The annoyance I felt when confronted with any object that didn't behave itself including sticking drawers was legendary; it was a weakness I had to get to grips with. I marvelled at the split second timing of this impression and I was sure that I was being politely told off! I joined a developing circle still desperate to see or hear something and the first night all I could think of was work mates from over twenty years ago; I had drawn a blank. I was asked their names and Rita, who I had never met before, had heard of most of them. She said that her late husband, who I didn't know, had worked for the same firm but not while I was at that branch and I didn't even know Rita's surname. This surely was not telepathy which would assume that she just happened to be thinking of the names of her husband's work mates from years before and that I had the ability to pick them up. There was also a phase when I would experience a dullness in my ears as though someone had put his or her hands over them, this usually indicated that I was saying or doing something wrong. I waited for the thought to tell me what; it never came. (It probably did but I have since learned how difficult it is to actively 'listen' for impressions.) I had either made a mistake or was just about to; I was short changed; I put the new letterbox on upside down; I was putting the back on a TV and the speaker leads had pulled off. When I started to put it down to some sort of self induced phenomena, and no less marvellous for that, it stopped. Sometimes I would experience a shrill whistle that seemed to go in one ear, right through my head and out through the other ear, probably because it was unimpeded! This most certainly meant, 'shut up.' Then they stopped happening. Now when I receive a tune it's a calling card from someone on the other side (verified through mediums.) - 'Charlie is my Darling' for Charles or 'Deutschland' for Friedrick. There might be a message, like, 'I never promised you rose garden', or 'happy talk', when I feel fed up with life 'Don't go changing when I desperately wanted to find a less stressful job. Of things to come I get, 'raindrops' or April showers when minor problems are imminent, or 'wonderful, wonderful, day', which always proves to be true against my worst expectations. (These indications often apply to tangible things like a repair.) I got 'These foolish things', as I used mam's microwave after her death and 'When I leave the world behind.' The tunes are always unexpected but the mind can and does produce some strange thoughts on its own account, I know that. Words picked up from Radio or TV sometimes stick in the mind also long-term memory will bring back what was originally given. At that point in time, at that age! I seemed to be able to remember if I had heard it somewhere, something I can't do now. I followed the example of my friend and colleague Frank and practiced inspired speaking. The doubts about its purity still remain to this day but because I am often surprised at the insightful content, it has given me confidence to publish 'The Spiritual Life' which is series of talks inspired to a greater or lesser degree by friends in spirit and referenced in this volume: I simply call it food for thought. For many years I sat with friends who had varying levels of sensitivity and wanted to develop their ability to get good proof. I made hard work of it with a few outstanding success and only fairly recently learned to recognise (at least some of the time) that still small voice that did not originate with me. During all of that time, now and again there would be sentences or words incoming whilst I was talking to someone or perhaps painting or gardening. Surveys suggest that a large percentage of the population hear 'voices' though I believe all of us do some being 'louder' than others and therefore more noticeable: Most assume that they are their own ideas. Our spirit friends make suggestions to help keep us on track throughout our lives and it's up to us if we choose to accept them. Some have found the voices extremely helpful but not all voices originate from good people and may be from individuals who are themselves disturbed, angry, nasty and even violent; also like attracts like; bad thoughts can attract bad companions. One of my original intentions in including the following horror stories was to impress the sceptic, assuming he or she has read thus far, and to show that you don't have to believe in electricity to receive a nasty shock. What we have read is bizarre-fantastic and hard enough to believe and what I am about to relate even more so. Bear in mind that barber Gordon Smith, a superb medium is not the

only one to say that he has encountered only *'benevolent beings'* during his many years practicing mediumship.
('Through My Eyes.' P22. Gordon Smith. Hayhouse. 2006.)

Opening the psychic door to any old passing spirit as in playing with the Ouija board or being obsessed with dark thoughts is not a good idea. Free will still operates after death so working mediums do have a guide or gatekeeper to prevent unwanted influences coming through. The most effective way of removing troublesome intrusions is to visualise being surrounded by pure white light, which is how some Spiritualists begin their circles. In the early days our *'guides'* constantly warned us against what they called playful spirits. Medium Stan Jones often made strong warnings about dabbling having had to deal with some quite nasty cases. Marlene Druhan is very experienced in out of body travel. – She categorises trouble makers as; *'Tricksters,'* who love to frighten people; *'Vicarious Spirits,'* with *'unresolved addictions or frustrations ...and will go to any lengths to influence a living person'* which can lead to *'exhaustion, illness and depression.'*
(P22-25. Naked Soul. Marlene Druhan Llewellyn 1998.)

Wilson Van Dusen, a clinical psychologist, examined thousands of mentally ill persons. He was able to strike up a relationship with some of the personalities the patients saw and heard. *'Most of them seemed fairly sensible except for their hallucinations, which invaded and interfered with their lives.'* ... *'For most individuals they ... came on suddenly.'* (P119) *'One woman was working in the garden when an unseen man addressed her. Another man described sudden loud noises he heard while riding on a bus; Most were frightened and adjusted with difficulty to this new experience. All the patients described the voices as having the quality of a real voice.'* ... *'Many suffer insults, threats and attacks for years from voices with no one around them being aware of it.'* Van Dusen learned that there were *'Lower-order voices similar to drunken bums at a bar who like to tease and torment just for the fun of it ...*(P121.)

Page 151

'In direct contrast stand the higher-order hallucinations ... perhaps a fifth or less of the patients experiences ... one man had heard the lower order arguing for a long while about how they would murder him. He also had a light come to him in the night like the sun. He knew it was a different order because the light respected his freedom and would withdraw if it frightened him ... This rare order seldom speaks whereas the lower order can talk endlessly. This higher order is much more likely to be symbolic, religious, supportive genuinely instructive; it can communicate directly with the inner feelings of the patient ... the higher order claims power over the lower order and, indeed shows it at times, but not enough to give peace of mind to most patients. (It) has indicated that the usefulness of the lower order is to illustrate and make conscious the patients' weaknesses and faults' ... 'a lady of the higher order was described as "an emanation of the feminine aspect of the Divine." When I implied she was divine she took offence. She herself was not divine but she was an emanation of the divine. (P125.)

('The Presence of Other Worlds.' Wilson Van Dusen. 1975.
   The findings of Emanuel Swedenborg. Wildwood House. 1 Wardour Street, London.)

I wondered if mental illness on occasion opens the psychic door however I was surprised at how many quite sane people do hear voices. The professionals refer to them as auditory hallucinations or even the normal process of a thinking mind. Surveys *support .. understanding voice-hearing as occurring on a continuum in the general population, and having meaning in relation to the voice-hearer's life experiences.*

(Journal of Mental Health 2011 Beavan, Read & Cartwright, Pub- Taylor & Francis)

Prof Richard Bentall has been very successful in helping sufferers deal with these unwelcome intrusions using CBT ('The Life Scientific' BBC Radio 4 Feb 2001) Only information that we couldn't normally have known about can indicate the difference between normal thinking and thoughts from spirit. It would seem that many problems are caused by very confused individuals not realising that they have passed over and are lost in their own thoughts of failure, guilt etc. Enmeshed in an individual's aura or energy field and totally bewildered they express themselves as if it were their own body manifesting as madness with the sufferer doing completely weird things. On the positive side I heard part of a BBC radio 4 programme on voice hearing one woman suddenly heard two voices telling her to go to hospital as she had a brain tumour. Obviously this was met with a great deal of scepticism however a doctor managed to persuade the hospital to scan her and she did indeed have a tumour: The voices then returned only to say that they were glad to be of help and left. When an architectural student in a deep fit of depression threw himself under a tube train in 1971 why did a complete stranger have a sudden irresistible urge to pull the communication cord, an act which saved the young man's life? Many writers and musicians have received full plots or scores into which little, if any, effort has been put whilst businessmen have their hunches and inventors their solutions. Now the power of the imagination is legendary, the human mind is bombarded with information from all directions and it is the nightmare of all writers that long forgotten words will find their way on to the page and they will be accused of plagiarism. But even some of these artists who have nothing to do with mediumship, sometimes feel the presence of their inspirer. When asked how she could produce so many plots each year for her famous love stories Dame Barbara Cartland replied that she simply prays for help. Sydney Sheldon said that the stories were given to him so quickly that he could scarcely get the words onto paper; he even felt the emotions of the characters. Sometimes what was imagined became true: Michael Bentine dreamed up a plot for his TV series 'Potty Time' which bore so many similarities to the storming of the Iranian embassy by the SAS, that it had to be postponed. On another occasion the most unusual thing he could think of, a donkey falling off a bridge, happened within a few days of putting pen to paper. (BBC Radio 4.) (P137 The Living Dream)

I wonder how much help is received by those who have discovered or invented cutting-edge technology. Perhaps that explains the eureka moment when the key to a problem is realised.

In the 'The Life Elysian' by R. J. Lees, there is an inspiring story of two small boys living on the streets of Victorian London. The elder boy, *'Dandy,'* dies leaving the younger boy, Bully Peg, penniless and starving. *'Dandy'* protests strongly that God was at fault somehow because he had not taken Bully Peg first. *'Myhanene,' 'Aphraar'* and *'Dandy'* go to help.- *'...In a flash of thought we found ourselves beside the hungry lad, who, with unshod feet and tattered clothes was doing his best to sell matches among the passers-by in front of the Royal Exchange.'* "Ere we is Bully," cried *'Dandy joyfully.* "Now yer can ha' some-" *'But his exclamation was cut short for the eager little fellow darted past him, without taking the slightest notice, in answer to a call for "Matches" from the top of a bus just pulling up at the kerbstone.'* "Well! If that don't tek the cake," gasped *'Dandy'*. "But p'raps 'e didn't see us in the fog." Then he added with an anxious sympathy, "Fogs don't do for Bully." *'Myhanene'* smiled and drew the little protector to him in a tender embrace which spoke more eloquently than words. "What are you laughing for?" He asked naively.
"At you thinking there is a fog," he replied. "You forget that you have changed your eyes and see what your friend cannot see, while he is not able to see that we are here. He started as he grasped an idea that had not occurred to him before.
"Yes. I forgot that! My eyes are dead uns, aint they? What shall we do?" His appearance was at once droll and pitiable. At length he realised what I had before seen-the apparent impassable gulf across which he wished to reach his friend.

"You must be satisfied for the present to let me do what I can to help your little friend," said 'Myhanene.' ... whilst I have come with you to let you see that Bully Peg has some breakfast, many other angels of God have gone away to bring someone here to give him what you wish and perhaps more than you expect. ... a Blackwell bus drew up, and a gentleman on the top was calling for matches, Bully dashed forward only to be encountered and pushed aside again by his more successful rival, and what was infinitely worse, his two remaining boxes of goods fell from his hand in the struggle under the moving wheel, ignited, and in a moment the broken hearted Bully was a hopeless bankrupt, without recourse or hope. As he looked at the blazing matches through his tears an elderly man cautiously stepped out of the 'bus and noticed him. "Here, here! What's the matter, what's the matter?" he enquired. It was not long before he understood the plight of this homeless orphan. "Now I know why the dear Lord put it into my heart to come to the city," (he said to himself.) (soon the man) 'was treating Bully Peg to a breakfast such as he had never faced before ... when the lad finished his meal, his friend took him eastward, where he knew he could find an ever open door for waifs and strays.' ('Myhanene' continued,) '"when I received my commission many other friends were sent forth to find servants of the Master whom they could impress to come to the Bank. Someone of the number will find a Christ-like soul who will be moved to respond. In some cases I have known two or even three to answer the premonition summon; but as soon as one sets out the fact is made known to the whole band of workers, who then relinquish their efforts with the many and concentrate their efforts on the one"... ('Aphraar' asked) '"Would it not be possible to foresee who would respond to the call and thus save what I may call an experiment with man?"' "That is, no doubt, foreknown to those who stand at a distance above and are not actually employed in the mission, But God never makes scant provision for the success of any service. Where omnipotence is available no result must be placed in

Page 155

jeopardy. Every agent employed knows that the mission cannot fail, but it requires energy, concentration and whole-hearted effort on our part, for no one of us can foresee how much our particular service affects the whole. Again these summonses to action serve to ascertain the value of the professions of those who pray to be used in the work of the Lord. Some men cry so loudly as to be unable to hear the still small voice calling them, and their lives pass by in workless praying. God has many devices for testing the genuineness of faith. '('The Life Elysian.' P193-5. RJ Lees. 1905)

Many people rely upon their own intuition as a spiritual being whereas a medium would have information impressed upon them by a spirit helper: Only by receiving evidence of an independent thinking mind can we assume that these thoughts and impressions are not influenced by our own ideas and prejudices. By impressing someone to give help to another person, our helpers are not interfering with free will as it is up to us whether or not we respond however it does seem to me that they do have a considerable influence on events. One day we ourselves might wish to become one of those helpers.

We work very hard to keep our charges on track, try to help them make the right decisions, come to the right conclusions and generally try to make life better despite the fact that things that go wrong can happen naturally: If it's a particular lesson to be learned we can't avoid that even though we want to. In all our dealings with human beings there is a lesson for us, seeing how people's minds work, how they ignore warning signs, how they take risks and how they generally are not self aware in certain respects and don't seem to have learned anything. So there are all kinds of strange conditions that the mind wrestles with and we play our part and try to correct, try to improve and try to amplify the good intentions. We try to help people to have a happier life because happiness is not a sin; we are all allowed a portion of it we cannot forever be down in the dumps or worrying about this or that. We try to help people

Page 156

to see a brighter future to see a good side of life and to be happy in their shoes. All of us have lessons to learn as I have said we are no exception and we learn by observing others and see how they react and by trying to understand the strange decisions they make. And all through life there is this decision making process going on and this is how we grow this is how we improve. When we make a mistake and we worry about it we make it bigger than it is but it is better to move on and see the other side of things: Sometimes a little laughter goes a long way. In your lives you have had many experiences, seen lots of people and observed how the different personalities react in different situations. You never can tell how people will respond to a call from us to help another person. Sometimes they will readily respond and go to that person's aid not realising that we have instigated that movement, that impulse. At other times there is doubt, something gets diverted and the person we want to help out is not there for us so sometimes we pick a second person if they are at hand to go and help out in a situation. All the time we are very busy we look forward to helping people and enjoy seeing when they respond taking our advice and moving on but other people have deaf ears and have to learn the hard way and so it is all through life: One great crowd of people helping, supporting and always being there and always there is help at hand and love in the air. (2019) *We cannot interfere where God would not allow. All is planned and there is a purpose behind all we say and do.* (2020

In the spirit worlds each individual gravitates to a place which is their natural mind set rather like the metaphorical Jacob's ladder, separating the progressed from the un-progressed. As we live our lives we have an affinity with certain regions of the spirit world therefore those who let their mind sink into muddy waters might attract individuals who could lead them into thought patterns from which it is hard to escape.

In our world we have the privilege of great teachers, souls who have passed through the shadow of the valley of death who have seen disturbing things but also joyous achievements, goals met, decisions made who are able to use their judgement and wisdom as we try to support and help our wards in their battle to survive, to understand, to grow in their journey through life. If we were to tell you of the many scenarios that we have been involved with it could take a very, very long time We come; we work; we impress; we help; we guide. And then we leave that we too might enjoy the fruits of our labours that we might discuss; compensate; over rule; turn the tables and generally use our influence to obtain a better outcome. And when we fail as sometimes we do when the forces of evil, or even the forces of nature are too strong for us we need to gather in our flock, help them through the process called death and bring them out into the light. (2019.)

'Behind 'H.J.L' stood a Great Spirit form made of light. His robes kept changing colour and seemed to run through all the colours of the rainbow. .. He was at least three times as large as 'HJL' and his face was more beautiful than any Greek sculpture-strong, noble, well-cut features- There was nothing feminine about it yet it was a kind as well as a strong face. It was a face that was neither old nor young. Nor did it seem to have colour as we understand it. but rather to be a figure of golden light. Yet there was both hair on his head and beard majestic and flowing. No words can describe the majesty and beauty of this being. I can quite understand where the ancients drew their inspiration for their Gods... (and when He spoke he spoke) with a glorious bell-like voice.'
(Gone West. P77. JSM Ward.B.A. Trance Vision/Auto Writing. Ryder.1918.)

A lot of people believe that 'angels' help them in daily life not realising that the answers come through their own thoughts and impressions some of which I have experienced including chance encounters. A TV or radio programme seen or heard at an exact moment; reaching for the very place where a particular book fallen behind the others in a book shop. My friend Stan Fowler rang the next day he was horrified when he realised that he had borrowed the same book a couple of years before. I said it doesn't matter I got another one yesterday. My first book brings into focus the wonderful work of these countless individuals that we call Angels. Some cultures pray to their ancestors which may seem to be something lesser than praying to God but in fact God is part of us. All levels might be co-opted when necessary especially so loved ones and friends with whom we have a bond. Surely they now have a perspective on life which in many cases is better than ours. A spirit has the ability to return as the character he/she once was, therefore a guide may adopt a persona that inspires his charge one guide calls it his astral wardrobe.

....since we were thought of as angels there has been a tendency to come clean about such apparitions, that we can ourselves manufacture and visualise ourselves in that role as we give inspiration and hope and lift spirits..(February 2020.)

Oliver Fox wrote:-
, 'I have talked with Masters in another world. I have seen-though from afar-Celestial Beings, great shapes of dazzling flame, whose beauty filled the soul with anguished longing.'
('Astral Projection.' P157. Oliver Fox. (Hugh George Callaway 1885 –1949) Rider. 1930)

Rosalind McKnight is told that we are all *'assigned'* a guardian angel and that when we need them they are *'instantly aware'*. As they live in a *'no-time existence'* *'They can perform a thousand tasks at once if necessary'* ...*'They are a completely different species and have never lived on earth.'....'They were ... created by God to be caretakers at all levels of creation'...'They are pure love and know no other emotions. They are collective energies of light... They can appear on earth temporarily* (and appear in) *human form to perform miracles. They are all powerful because they are moulded out of spirit which is pure love.*
(P120-121 'Soul Journeys.' Rosalind McKnight. Hampton Roads. 2005.)

In our world we have many different scenes; scenarios; conditions; many loving moments; all kinds of things to delight the heart and when we are taking ourselves seriously we enjoy that too: Having a good chin wag, opening up old memories; discussing and analyzing and we have a wonderful time. Then we come down to earth's conditions which can be quite challenging but never-the-less it's a challenge that makes our lives worthwhile; we love what we do; we love the people we work for; and we love each other. In time there are many things to challenge us as spirits, as men and women always there is a new angle, a new outlook, something to come to terms with but how could life be any different if we were constantly going over the same old ground; seeking the familiar without looking forward to the new; the exciting; the daunting perhaps. And so change is the stuff of life always something going on always new things to delight us; to make us think; to test our mettle. Friends old and new coming and returning and meeting again, coming into our aura and discussing how much we have changed in the interim: How differently we look at the world how differently we look at the lives we have lived and see them in a different light. For this is one of the beauties of reincarnation to be able to see with different eyes; to see ourselves as others see us; to understand where we went wrong; what we were thinking when we chose a particular course. And so there are always lots of things to occupy our minds to keep us busy and to keep us occupied. In spirit there are great souls, loving souls who look down upon us trying to shed their light upon us and make us better than we are; to help us to appreciate life in all its glory; to shine through the gloom; to hold out the hand of hope, of love and friendship. Always these shining lights are there and always they help mankind through his difficulties and his problems and they try to make the going a little easier for why should we suffer unnecessarily? Giving you all these thoughts is a way of helping you understand that we are real people we are very involved in things we are not some mystical or magical force which comes with a magic wand to make everything all right. To put things in perspective we are working people who are friends; who are neighbours we are all kinds of things to each other and we wish you so much well in your life to make a success of it; to be at one with your friends and your colleagues and your loved ones and to appreciate each other as we often didn't do in our lives because we were so sheltered, and so naive about lots of things. Now when mankind thinks he knows everything it really highlights the things that he doesn't know, the things that are important like friendship, like understanding people who are out of line out of step with everybody else, to try to see how they tick and try to give them help rather than locking them up or shutting them out of our minds. In the spirit world we see all things, and we understand all things and so we try to shed some light for your little circle and for your friendship and love that binds us together.

(October 2019)

...love must be shared to be appreciated, in our world we have constant feelings of comradeship, love of our fellows, and an at oneness, special relationships which are the foundation of reality: Not separate but not joined either, we are our own master, we use our will, our decision making, our own conclusion. Our experiences are all our own and yet we share and share alike... (Jan 2020)

In your minds you have many hopes and wishes and fears too and we want you to set about putting them in order that you might anticipate only the best, that you might feel the purpose and the pleasant longing for all things spiritual. In your minds there is great power and great potential and yet you neglect to use that power; you anticipate only the bad and the negative. In our world thoughts take shape; we come to you on wings of thought, we drive our chariots by the power of thought, everything we do is moulded by thought and yet you in your world are inclined to let thoughts take care of themselves. It is a power that is there to be used, to shape and mould, to increase your potential,

Page 161

to direct your own body, your own wishes and your desires. In the world of man there is a tendency to follow the dictates of the material, to let the day rule your mind instead of letting your mind rule the day: To look on brighter and fairer thoughts which will permeate through your body, which will radiate to other people and bring an atmosphere which is uplifting and which is worthy of the spiritual. And these thoughts must be cultivated so that you have only good thoughts, pleasant thoughts and positive thoughts in anticipation of something that you are building which is a power; a strength; a unity and an agreement to go forward together. And in that power to hold a reservoir for when things are not so good you can draw from it and make it yours. For there is strength in numbers and together you will succeed and with your friends in the world of spirit who send you their loving thoughts, and their power too, you will create a mighty force. The real world beckons; leave behind the world of shadow, the world of dreams, take hold of the reins and fly on the wings of love. These thoughts I give to you with my love and my best wishes. God bless. ('The Spiritual Life' 2016. January 1995.)

'Elliotson' controlling:- The return to earth is a great trial for me. I might compare it to the descent from a pure and sunny atmosphere into a valley where the fog lingers. In the atmosphere of earth I seem completely changed. The old habits of thought awaken, and I seem to breath a grosser air.' (P16/17. 'More Spirit Teachings.' Stainton Moses. Psychic Book Club. 1952.)

In the world there are many ills, many setbacks, many tragedies and these we have to take in our stride we cannot be distracted from the work we do we cannot involve our own feelings or memories which would take us onto a different wavelength and not allow us to do our jobs and so we have to be very focused we have to look carefully at what we are doing and the things we are thinking and try to concentrate very hard to bring about that change in understanding, that link with those that we love and those that we care for. (3rd Feb 2020)

VIRTUAL REALITY

At the moment virtual reality machines are in their infancy but by donning headgear and gloves etc, you can become part of a computer programme. Perhaps eventually we will be able to plug in mentally, with a combination of sights, sounds and feelings and under induced hypnosis we could really live the part, and experience what it was like to be Napoleon, or good Queen Bess. All of this isn't so farfetched but within the bounds of possibility as man will take the virtual out of reality and the images will be three dimensional with smells and textures. Instead of having to play against a simple image of a man or monster responding to the variables of the programme we might have to pit our wits against characters that are thinking computers within the computer. The game would not be switched off when it became too difficult or boring and would be played to its conclusion but like life itself there would be levels and at the end of one we would begin another perhaps as a new character in a new life. If, somewhere in the Universe, there was a technology which was at our present stage countless billions of years ago, it would be sure to have perfected virtual reality for entertainment or learning. What man can do perhaps God did first. 'Joe' on BBC1's 'Eastenders' said that someone had died and gone to heaven and found that God was a teenager playing with his game boy. According to an article in the New Scientist what we call reality might actually be the output of a program running on a cosmos-sized quantum computer. (New Scientist. 26 September 2012. Michael Brooks)

Man may never travel to the ends of the universe but he can contain it all within his own imagination; one day it might be possible to hold that information within an artificial memory and display it on one small TV screen. Perhaps creation is like a mighty, three-dimensional computer screen, where the vast distances and immense complexity of the Universe have been memorized; time and distance are nothing but an illusion. Scenes from the past, the present or the future can be selected from the memory and displayed instantly, as the operator so desires. A computer can manipulate images and create and change shapes, it can give the impression of flying through space, and so on like life in the dream and spiritual worlds. Computers with their menus, files, and back up memories might be compared with the various strata of human consciousness: Death is merely a click of the mouse, a different file, a different screen a different vibration. Thinking of reality as being like a computer with its way of manipulating images and accessing files makes anything seem possible. –

Richard Bower at Durham University in the UK and his colleagues have created a computer simulation approximately 1 billion light years across, which models tens of thousands of galaxies. (New Scientist 2019)

Who would ever have thought that a line of written code could be converted into a three dimensional object by a printer? Is this the precursor to 'Beam me up Scotty' or even the film 'The Fly' where the inventor hadn't bargained for the computer reading the information from a fly in the cabinet and blending it with the person waiting to be beamed up? Needless to say the result was quite horrific. We may think of computers as eventually being able to display intelligence way beyond that of a human being, in truth I doubt they can ever match the staggering complexity of the human body, sprouted from the dead earth like the fruit of the field where everything that enables it to understand what surrounds it is displayed on that one small screen inside the head. I am not however suggesting that our virtual reality is based in the material worlds and that we are laid out on a bed somewhere having this experience. Our present reality is an integral part of our own being which it seems is created and experienced by mind. Perhaps we have an unconscious awareness of other dimensions far beyond the cranium where only mind can penetrate.

WORDS ON THE PAGE.

Used as I am to experiencing the unbelievable I am more than satisfied with the evidence for survival but when it comes to the ultimate questions like who made God and why is there anything at all we are seeing the picture through the prism of human minds. In this volume all names of communicators are printed in quotes and Italics: Because the words have been transmitted through the active mind of the writer it's impossible to be sure that they have not been altered in any meaningful way. I have no doubt that many of the ancient religious and philosophical writings have been inspired by spirit but when we are looking for basic facts about creation how can we know if there is any truth to be found even if only metaphorical. One could ask where did the idea originate of an invisible after-death world with its Gods and angels so real that some cultures thought they could take their servants and their riches with them. Perhaps it was an attempt to explain lucid dreaming or out of body experiences, maybe a more common practice in the early days: In the spirit world surroundings might have appeared to be an idealised version of their ordinary life.

The prophets were inspired with tales or parables, which would get complicated truths accepted in the thinking of the day: Simple stories which were taken literally or possibly mistranslated. This would catch the imagination and would stand the test of time but were taken as real events and once engrained in society through tradition would be difficult to supplant. The hands through which these writings passed were many and varied and meanings were unintentionally changed during translation and selection: Then various Christian Saints were given the impossible task of deciding which stories would be included in the Bible drawing upon all kinds of unverifiable sources.

According to inscriptions on the Catacombs. *"The early Christians speak of the dead as though they were still living.*

They talk to their dead." There' is nothing of a blood sacrifice (or) a virgin birth.' A predominant symbol 'is that of the Good Shepherd. Prior to the Nicene Council St Augustine says that the spirits of the dead can unveil the future to the living and 'refers to practices...which enable a person to communicate with spirits.' After the council of Nicaea. St Clement of Alexandria and St Jerome made similar claims.

(Psychic News May 19 2001. from 'The History of Spiritualism, Vol. 2'
by Sir Arthur Conan Doyle.)

History tells of many Gods including self-appointed Roman Emperors and Egyptian Queens. The willingness to deify certain individuals, some of whom *were* probably exceptional, was common and often stories about them seem to be a re-telling of episodes in the lives of previous 'saviour gods': Perhaps also there were spirits who wished to exert their own power. Belief has had a major role in all societies for example an important change relevant to mediums was added to the King James Bible *'Thou shall not suffer a witch to live'* We all know the horror that was inflicted on many innocent people but despite these contradictions and man-made alterations it contains wonderful philosophy, history and plenty of fascinating stories. At this point, thinking of other religions, I remember the words of Frank's *'guide'* when asked a certain question, his answer was,

"I am not here to discuss which representative of the divine is the greatest." (*Guides* of course come from all religions.) Fellowship and striving to be a better person is common to most religions but sadly these words on the page, peppered with man's misinterpretations, became something to argue about and still cause a great amount of conflict and misery. Even information from 'the dead' may not be reliable as there are countless partitions and points of view in the spirit world certainly at lower levels. Each of us has our own beliefs and way of looking and describing things for instance when out of the body or having a personal experience. Those who desperately want to get at the truth

Page 166

are sure to doubt the witnesses and want to see for themselves. They may wonder if there is a God why He does not make things clearer and when someone is really suffering they sometimes turn to God but-

...(some) people say that they feel nothing but a void, an emptiness, a longing for God, and yet not a sign not a miraculous appearance, nothing to signify that the prayers, the pleading has been heard but let me assure you that every word is accounted for, is listened to, is responded that that person may find peace in different way, not always obvious, not always coming with bells and trumpets, but silently, coming into the mind, making changes which will bring the sufferer out into the light, and into a new phase for God is not unkind, suffering is not a part of the plan rather a side effect caused by those other factors which human beings encounter in a life on earth and in the process of living... (August 2020)

In the world of man there is that brotherhood which is unseen and unrecognized where one helps another in the name of God without even knowing (17th August 2020)

If we believe that there is no God will we become selfish and immoral? The humanists say not. The maze of existence with its countless hidden meanings, experiences and twists and turns, beginnings and ends is an essential ingredient of living and exploring: It is a challenge, an industry, a rich subject for artists, writers and thinkers, an opportunity to weigh the evidence and advance our understanding. There are strands in many religions which would fit well with this book though often distorted as in the cast system so some what may be called facts have managed to filter through. If God is in the mix we might go to the ends of the earth and not find Him all the while being surrounded by His presence and the visible evidence of a truly superior intelligence.

TIME.

Altogether the strangest issue is to do with time not just in comparison to other beings which may exist in other worlds but in a really mind boggling way. This subject goes hand in hand with 'Precognition' which demonstrates that the future is there before we have experienced living it.

What is the nature of time will it ever come to an end can we go back in time? Someday these answers may seem as obvious to us as the earth orbiting the sun or perhaps as ridiculous as a tower of tortoises; only time, whatever that may be, will tell
(Stephen Hawking 'The Theory of Everything.' A Benoit Delhomme. Film 2014.)

In his dreams and visions Emanuel Swedenborg (1689-1772.) claimed to have spoken with angels who have no notion of time. To one such person he spoke *'as man with man.' 'At first he did not know what it was that I called time, so I was obliged to inform him fully about it.'* Swedenborg explained about the earth and the sun and how the calendar was calculated. *'On hearing this he was much surprised, and said that he knew nothing of such things, but he knew what states were.'* (P107. 'Heaven and Hell.' Swedenborg Society.)

Time on earth is dictated by the rotation of the earth and the necessity to work and sleep at regular intervals. We see that life is about events in sequence that must surely take time but if everything is in the now would we have a memory capable of containing the whole of eternity or is there perhaps an 'external' memory? Some say that there is and refer to it as *the Akashic records which are, in some New Age circles, held to be a mystical, otherworldly compendium of all knowledge. The word "akashic" derives from the Sanskrit "akasha", meaning "sky" or "space". Some even call it the "mind of God". It has been used in mysticism since the nineteenth century.* (TV Tropes.com.)

This sounds similar to Carl Jung's mass subconscious or a single absolute mind, a transcendent intelligence.

In spirit, time is purely a mental experience, astral travellers who feel that they have been over for hours are surprised when they find that they have been out of the body for only a short time. Apparently some individuals are trapped in their own little world immediately after death and remain unaware of time passing until rescued. Sometimes this can be many years as we count time but to them it seems that only a few hours have passed therefore. Is the phrase *'A thousand years are like one day to God'* ancient knowledge or creative thinking? (Moses. Psalm 90 The Bible.)

Fredrick Sculthorpe spent *'a week's holiday with* (his) *wife in spirit- in one night.'* (P93.) Though he did find that *'the dull astral localities seem to have a kind of time in regard to the duration of an activity that is nearer to our earthly state.'* ('Excursions to the Spirit World.' P94. Fredrick Sculthorpe)

One lady said that her near-death experience *'lasted one second or that it lasted ten thousand years and it wouldn't make any difference how you put it.'''*
('The Light Beyond.' P14. Raymond & Moody Jr., M. D.' & Paul Perry. Pan 1981.)

(Sir)'Oliver Lodge' claimed that *'five earthly nights correspond to five or even fifty years in our world.'*
(Nobody Wants to Listen. P42. ConPsy Publications. Raymond Smith.)

'H.J.L.' was in division one for a few days that seemed to him like years. (Gone West. P36. JSM Ward. Ryder 1913.)

Whilst Psychic News Editor and medium for *'Silver Birch'* *'Maurice Barbanell,'* said it was difficult to judge time at all (P27.) and found that one could be in two time phases at once *'with more consciousness of the future time level.'*
('The Barbanell Report.' P158. Paul Beard & Marie Cherrie. Pilgrim Books. 1987.)

There are claims that a whole lifetime can seem to those in spirit like a few days. (Sylvia Browne) *'Veronica'* who speaks through trance medium April Crawford and calls herself *'A nonphysical Causal Plane Entity and guide,'* often refers to our existence as *'life in the linear.'*
(*'Veronica'* through April Crawford www.InnerWhispers.net.)

OF MANY LIVES.

Reincarnation was very nearly part of Christian beliefs, the doctrine of the pre-existence of the soul was outlawed by the Council of Constantinople in 553AD by I believe one vote. The Pope and many important Bishops did not attend.

It tickles my imagination to think that a soldier who died alone in a first-world-war fox-hole is now a modern teenager riding a skate board skilfully down the street to the sound of his (or her) smart phone, or that a Roman Centurion may be operating a till in Tesco's. Perhaps the old woman who lived and died in poverty, looking after ten children, and scraping a meagre living from the land, her world composed of the few square miles around the village, is now a bright young executive at Marks and Sparks. - A Klu Klux Clan leader might be born as an African in order to learn to love the people he once hated and an unjust judge is in jail for a crime he didn't commit.

The idea, the advantage of living a human life is well known, but before it can take place there is much planning and soul searching. There are even points in a lifetime where we may exit or not as in a narrow escape

During regressive hypnosis adopted subjects claimed that they were born to be, not with their natural parents but with their adoptive ones.

('Life Before Life.' Helen Wambach. Bantam Books. 1979.)

Brigitte Rix's '*guide*':- "*The soul is like a mirror we look at when we look at you. We see your soul not your body. In your soul, we see your lives before this one,* **or after**, (My emphasis) *or all mixed up, all superimposed! If you wish us to be able to contact you and stay in tune with you, we need that life which is 'now' for you, to remain present in the mirror. ...'a clear and quiet Mind absolutely still,'*

(P32Vol 2 I'm not dead I'm alive' Brigitte Rix. Cons Psy.2013.)

Rosalind A. McKnight is told that, "*... all souls are living in all lifetimes in the timeless dimension, but are*

experiencing them from the time dimension as if they were happening one at a time."
(P168. Cosmic Journeys. Rosalind A. McKnight. Hampton Roads. 1999.)

I visualised lives one after the other flowing like a river whilst someone outside of that time frame could look at it from above with each life influencing the next but. Robert Monroe was told that living two lives simultaneously takes place frequently and was even given the name and location and yet hadn't the courage to face this other self.
('Far Journeys.' P270. Robert Monroe Doubleday. 1985.)

The implications of this are staggering, is this other self someone who we would look up to or someone we would despise, or even hate! The Dali Lama claims that just as a moon can remain in the sky and yet be reflected *'in placid lakes and seas,'*...'a *Buddha may incarnate simultaneously in many different bodies'*. Asked if he could remember any of his previous lives he said *"at the moment no"* but that when he was around three or four he used to speak a dialect which was not of his birthplace and had *'showed the search party'* that he 'knew about' (his) *'previous incarnation'.*
(P150/151. 'Reincarnation.' Vicki Mackenzie. Bloomsbury. 1988.)

This returns us to the 'fragmented self,' our individuality which is me which is you: The question of how we can live other lives in the same time frame is certainly food for thought. April Crawford's guide *'Veronica'* even claims that *You can be born in the year 2000, pass out of that life in 2020, become reborn in 1752.* I am staggered by this.

When I began to research this subject a lot of Spiritualists didn't seem to believe in Reincarnation including certain *'spirit guides'*: now I think I can see why. It seems that on the lower spirit planes we may not have become aware of our other lives therefore some of those who communicate with mediums will tell a different story. As we return to earth's environment from the spirit worlds old memories return. Apparently it is our spirit that garners all information and as we progress in the spirit world we will learn a lot by seeing things from different viewpoints.

Page 171

When I look at babies I imagine an adult born with a completely blank slate; no memories with which to understand this strange experience. We also have a gene pool from which the habits, appearance and structure of the body emerges. Certain amazing abilities seem to be built in or programmed for many living beings, generally called instinct. In order to learn new things, be with a family, achieve certain goals or re-visit old weaknesses we are a selected part of our total self and to a large extent a blank canvas, a different person from birth: This will hopefully insulate us from terrible things *we* may have done in the *past* but that may not be wholly true. It is said that echoes of our previous life are with us until about seven. It made me wonder about those who feel that they are in the wrong gender but apparently it seems to be more about new experiences. According to 'Seth'- ...*Since all events occur at once ...there is little to be gained by saying that a past event causes a present one*...(Because) *The whole self is aware of all the experiences of all of its egos.... There are bound to be similarities between them and shared characteristics.*

(P150 Conversations with Seth by Susan Watkins, Moment Point Press 2005)

The evidence seems to suggest that those who die young may reincarnate as the same consciousness with some memory and physical scars from the life cut short, at least in the early years. When I was very small I recall barking at the other kids "left right left right" as I tried to get them into line. I remember lying in bed thinking that I had to have Polio to prevent me from going into the army again. Thoughts on such weighty questions that this book is considering never entered my head until I was nearly thirty.

If the future is already there would that mean we are trams not busses and free will would merely be an illusion; not a hopeful thought. Surely just because someone up ahead can see the results of our choices does not mean that we don't have the free will to make them. If we could choose to live the life of Henry the Eight would it be like re-living a play or film, like plugging in a flash drive containing the memory of that life into a computer? Would Henry have had free will, did he create that drama? Is my life an illusion, an action replay or the original? Whilst I can accept that we could perhaps re-live the *memory* of a life lived even by a different spirit I'm not sure that it would be possible in the physical sense but how would we know! To add to the confusion when some claim that we can live multiple versions of the *same* life or that someone can take over another's life halfway through it begins to seem even more complicated and unlikely and my interest wanes; but I guess anything is possible. Apparently choosing to return to an earlier date is less common as most individuals are a part of a group who move forward together. There are however plenty of reports which indicate that a life can be shaped and moulded in certain essentials before it is lived.

'Albert Pauchard' says that *'here'* ... *we* ... *'create the models' of what will be achieved physically during our next incarnation - at least as far as material conditions will permit.* ('The Other World.' P143. Pelegrin Trust. Pilgrim Books. 1952.)

Betty Eadie told Oprah that during her N.D.E, She saw beings of light *"preparing to come to earth selecting their body and their life situation. Some had chosen bodies that were mentally handicapped as well as physically deformed, others chose perfect bodies and perfect situations."* Oprah asked why they would choose dysfunctional families. Betty said that *"they were the greater spirits who came to earth to help bring true love or to help those on the earth to love."* She said that the spirits who had selected their birth were, *"very eager, very happy."*
(Betty Eadie. Author of 'Embraced by the Light.'
The Oprah Winfrey Show. Channel 4 Television.)

Paul Elder is told by *'Meldor'* – *'Our teachers have told us that we began as part of one great consciousness. In order to experience diversity and to honour ever continuing creation, we, as parts of the Creator, agreed to become individuated and split off from the source. By doing so the All, which you refer to as God could experience itself in endless evolving form and reality....what we experience as* *individuated beings, seemingly in isolation, is actually also experienced by <u>the All</u> at various levels of understanding and consciousness.* (P126.) *'...the essence of God ... is the universal energy of Love...essentially the energy vibration of all souls.'* (P96 'Eyes of an Angel' Paul Elder, Hampton Roads. 2005.)

Life in all its forms is a harmony of God's thoughts. In every aspect of living there is a contribution towards the whole and this is the climbing of the ladder towards the highest heavens. (1990 The Spiritual Life 2016. Michael Featherstone Amazon.)

'Myers' complicates things even more. *'We will not be born again.'* We can cope with that bit but then he says, *'... a new soul, one who will join our group, will shortly enter into the pattern of Karma I have woven for him on earth.'* Fair enough but he makes it sound as though the previous individuals that were ME, exist as separate people instead of compartments in MY memory. It would seem that being in two minds can be taken literally. He compares *'certain centers in the brain'* with the *'number of souls all bound together by one spirit.'* He says that *'there may be contained within that spirit twenty souls, a hundred souls, a thousand souls. The number varies. It is different for each man.'* *'We are all of us distinct, though we are influenced by others of our community on different planes of being.'*
(P69-72.'The Road to Immortality.' Geraldine Cummins. Psychic Press. 1932.)

......we as spirits have a tremendous responsibility for we are in effect creating a new individual who will have to bear the weight of the things that we have planned and although it is us it is a separate individual too so we have to think long and hard about our progress and where we need to go and how we need to deal with it......(September 2020.)

Is this the answer to the multiple personality syndrome or are they simply helpers of which most are normally unaware? The spirit is like a diamond and each of us is a facet constantly being polished to make it perfect. Another example is of a cart wheel, the spirit is the hub and each spoke is an individual life presumably with shared characteristics.

Brigitte's mum again:- - I had to go *'within myself'* asking *"Where is the real Whole Me'?"* *Then I saw pictures unfurl in front of me, others superimposed over them and I realised there were many different 'ME' aspects I was unaware of...'...It's exciting...to see yourself as someone you did not know'* (P200)   *'It was a shock to see myself as another woman and as a man, yet my inner characteristics were not so different.!'* (P201) *I saw a man of long ago, who was 'me'! He still exists and his spirit is part of my 'Higher Self' as* **he is one of my facets.** *Yet he has not finished living his life; he continues to do so in thoughts, fancy that! He feels as who he was and has been thinking that way for a long time. He has only begun to realise that he was not just what he knew himself as!*(I'm Not Dead I'm Alive.' P276.Vol. 2 Brigitte Rix)

Myers continued:- I lived two lives, one in the world of form, and one subjective, in the community of which I am a member'. 'I am, therefore, a kingdom, and yet I am but a unit in that kingdom'. (P62/64) *'The Soul-man, however may not leave .. for the Sixth plane until the group soul is complete, until those other souls, necessary to this design woven into the tapestry of eternity, have also attained to this level of consciousness.'* (P69/70.) In exceptional cases, *'for a lofty purpose,'* (some) *'descend once again into matter. They are not strong enough to make the great leap into timelessness, they are not yet perfect.'* (P73.) Those who are tired of the world of things and desire to move upwards onto the fifth plane become aware of the individual parts of the group soul, parts of the one unifying spirit which includes *'plants, trees, flowers, birds, insects, fish, beasts, men and women; representatives of living creatures in varying states of evolution ... on various planes, various levels of consciousness in the After-Death. ... creatures on other planets.'*   On the sixth plane there comes the *'unifying of all those mind units I have called souls within the spirit.'* Eventually in the seventh state there is the

passage from the material universe almost into formlessness: An... *'individual'...* and yet at *'one with God.'*
(P69-72.'The Road to Immortality.' Geraldine Cummins. Psychic Press. 1932.)

'Elliotson' through Stainton Moses ...Some of the higher spirits have lost their identity and have become *a center of influence. The exalted sprit, 'Imperator' who directs this medium bathes me in his influence.* (P16 More Spirit Teachings)

........all kinds of things do we masquerade as which are part of our experience; part of our long history and we can turn our hand to many things so when we come to you we can infuse you with whatever it is that you need; joy; happiness; thoughtfulness; putting the brakes on, preventing you from taking a line of thought which is harmful to you, yourself or others.........' (March 2020)

I have just been listening to a discussion between two scientists about the idea that inanimate objects are conscious. My take on it would be that I am aware of my finger but my finger isn't aware of me.
(Galileo's Error. Foundations for a New Science of Consciousness Philip Goff Nov 2019)

The life that each of us lives is unique, not a copy not a re-run but an original, to say that they all run in parallel is a misnomer They do run sequentially but like a river one can go back to an earlier stage and re-live. Everything that is said and done remains constant, in abeyance, suspended in space until activated. When the consciousness becomes aware of it, it becomes real and then it is re-lived, re-imagine, recovered so whilst previous lives may in a sense be before this one in another sense they never die, the power is there, the visions, the thoughts and the feelings all accredited to each individual but in reality placed there before the dawn of man in a kind of imagined tableaux that can be manipulated and changed according to the will of the one experiencing it. It is actually a difficult concept to grasp because is a question of which came first the chicken or the egg when in fact both happened simultaneously.

(November 2020.)

ETERNITY AND CONCLUSIONS.

"The important thing is not to stop questioning."
Albert Einstein.

In the spirit world there are many sides to everything. You will never really reach the bottom of things because they are so deep and so complex and so wonderful. What would it be like if we knew everything, if there was nothing to search for nothing to ponder on, to imagine? And so we've got plenty of material to keep us busy for eternity. (Sept 2019)

So much exists that has not been discovered. It certainly does not mean that it does not exist.....always step back to observe the big picture in any experience
('*Veronica*' through April Crawford. (Trance) Inner Whispers September 2020)

The 'technology' of eternity if I can call it that is bound to be so far in advance of anything we could even imagine. To accept that our universe has its origins in a completely different reality must be a personal decision. What we have read so far is fascinating, weird, and has more questions than answers but truth is stranger than fiction. Keeping in mind the insubstantiality of the mighty universe and everything that exists; the digital cloud; the possibility of worlds within worlds and the question of the feasibility and indeed the reality of a life after death: Was the process of survival of the fittest a free-running programme with all of the ingredients carefully placed like a domino rally and has there been involvement in that design since the beginning? Is there more to a human being than science can detect, are we simply our memory and if we have a soul what does that really mean? Does hypnosis tell us anything about how we perceive our world, are some dreams a glimpse of reality and do our senses tell us the truth? Are coincidences and lucky breaks a sign of some sort of underlying control or pattern? What about seeing events which haven't happened yet and things that go bump in the night? These questions must surely influence the way we look at our existence. The one thing that science teaches us is that everything works by pure logic. By manipulating the building blocks of matter, science is showing us what wonders are possible using the laws of Physics, which are after all the laws of the Universe: How did such an infinitely complex system come into existence? We think of the human being with his great intelligence as being the crowning glory of evolution but the brain; the eyes; the memory and that TV screen inside our heads existed many millions of years before cameras; television and computers were even dreamed of at a time when animals were said to be primitive: Perhaps then the 'design' is itself evidence of an infinitely greater intelligence. I look upon the human body as a spectacular example of bio engineering and programming and we can see more and more that other living things, beings at the bottom of the evolutionary scale such as birds; small animals; even insects, far from being curious adornments, have a will and an awareness of their own. Some people believe that we began existence as minerals and gradually climbed the ladder of consciousness through plant, insect, fish and animal as part of a group soul before entering a more advanced body.

Like many invertebrates, spiders were assumed to be little more than automata, without an inner life. Yet research has now revealed that they possess hidden cognitive abilities rivalling those of mammals and birds. These include complex learning, foresight and planning, and even the capacity to be surprised. Stranger still, spider silk turns out to be so important to the cognitive abilities of these arachnids that some scientists believe it should be considered part of their mind. ('New Scientist.' Feb 2020.)

Mice convey a range of emotional states with their facial expressions, including pleasure, disgust and fear
(CNN. New Scientist April 2020)

Birds have in-built navigation systems and snails the ability to find their way home after being thrown into somebody else's garden! The technical wizardry of nature far surpasses anything science can make at the moment therefore how do we feel about this? Everything is so delicately organised, but what if, for example, elephants had the brain power of humans without the dexterity to create things?

It's so difficult to separate opinions from scientific fact, the word 'creation' is like a massive insurmountable road block in our thinking even though here we are living in this world with wondrous impossibilities all around us. There is a fear of looking or feeling foolish and so we call it 'mother nature,' turn away and think of something else but of course that leaves us where we are; accepting this weird, wonderful and sometimes terrifying life as it is; what more can we do? Think of the inventiveness of man in a relatively miniscule period of time but imagine what could be discovered in an eternity with endless inventions and designs overlaid one upon another.

'The creation of the world was not instantaneous but a project which was developed over many eons of time as the universe took shape and the minds in charge, in control, developed, changed, thought deeply and visualized all that is. (December 2019)

But why should this force from which everything material has originated, be chained to it forever like some genie in a bottle, why should it build for itself a prison house of matter? The answer of course is all of the drama and wonder of life: Living is big business it occupies the minds of the 'living' and the 'dead' Without it we would be bland; featureless; meaningless; hollowed out; useless beings not able to cope on our own; not able to bring others joy let alone ourselves, and being always faced by a bleak and a bland existence

"Space," it says, "is big. Really big. You just won't believe how vastly, hugely, mind bogglingly big it is. I mean, you

Page 179

may think it's a long way down the road to the chemist's, but that's just peanuts to space."

('Hitchhikers Guide to the Galaxy.' Douglas Adams.)

Considering the impossibility of anyone or anything creating our vast universe I looked at the idea of relativity; that other living beings somewhere in time and space could be having an entirely different experience to human beings. We simply don't know how big the universe is. Whilst our body is miniscule in comparison, our imagination doesn't do size or distance or even time therefore if mind is all anything is possible. We think in terms of scientific laws but if mind represents the power behind creation then presumably it can imagine anything it wishes: It created the laws and can change, modify or even abolish them. According to Medium Rosemary Brown, *'Bertrand Russell'* commented that the longer he was over there the more he was inclined to believe that anything was possible.

I tried to visualize the structure of everything we see around us in terms of the world of the atom; an insubstantial world where there is plenty of room for unseen energies; infra red and ultra violet light; gasses; radio and television signals. Some physicists postulate other dimensions; worlds within worlds interleaved like television channels co-existing 'side by side' in the same space like the countries at the opposite ends of the globe that were once waiting to be *'discovered.'*

Alan Kardec's sources say that *"the soul may live many lives on the same globe if it not be sufficiently advanced to pass into a higher one."* There are, they say, worlds that are so advanced and the physical body so much less dense as to be nearer the spiritual worlds than the physical within which we live on earth. Each new life brings them further up the ladder towards the spiritual with the spiritual and physical worlds *"blending into one another as the darkness of night melts into the dawn."*

('The Spirits' Book.' 1857. P72-76. Alan Kardec. (L,.D,.H,.Rivail.) Psychic Press.)

Perhaps this means that apparently dead planets might be surrounded by life which is invisible to our eyes.

If creation is the result of a free running program could a virus or a major disaster wipe out mankind, if it is foreseen, will the powers that be limit its scope?

The earth in all its glory shall not fail, there will be new and exciting changes; something to ponder on; to make life better, to address some of the imperfections in man's thinking; make him more aware of his responsibilities; teach him to be kinder and more considerate; putting forth new shoots into the spiritual world and when they do there will be new lessons to learn as the two worlds blend together as one. This is the ultimate goal, the future for which mankind is destined; not annihilation; not pain and suffering; but a calm and peaceful world; an optimistic world; thoughtful; creative and expansive. In the future men will traverse the universe but in a different form, not in a flesh body but a spiritual body, an idea; a proposal which will allow explorers to investigate the far reaches of the universe. It is an exciting prospect far, far away into the future but when these things are happening there will be an awakening that I spoke of, there will be that understanding. To you it is in the far distant future to us it is ever present.

(Feb 2020)

Speaking to Paul Beard via Marie Cherrie, *'Maurice Barbanell,'* (tells us that in the spirit world) *'it's a strange thing this reality. You've got to realise constantly that you'll only see what you want to see and so you've to make a conscious effort to broaden the field and sometimes you are seduced by seeing what you want to see.'* (P12) *(I'm) amazed at the number of people who have been over here for some time and who show no inclination to learn or to become more aware.'* (P15) *'It's much more exciting than I expected, the possibilities are endless and quite daunting.'.* (with a). *'tremendous sense of well being, you feel you could move mountains.'* (P16) *There are periods when I cannot remember what I have done or where I have*

Page 181

been. (P27) *Many times in the past I too doubted when others communicated but now ... I realise the problems others who came before me had in coming out with irrefutable evidence.* (P30)

('The Barbanell Report.' Paul Beard & Marie Cherrie. Pilgrim Books. 1987.)

During out-of-body and near-death experiences our world can look transparent like the projector beams in a smoky cinema as if we are the ghosts. Our physical world is for most of us fixed and stable whilst out of the body there is the tendency to hallucinate objects and places which can be mixed with real events for instance when the subject meets someone they didn't know had died until they return to the body. It seems to have more in common with dreams and yet it is often said that it is so vividly real that it makes our everyday life look like a sleep walk. Subjects find themselves in a world where mind is king, thoughts take shape, they feel at one with the landscape and anything is possible. I began by making my investigation in an evidential, sensible way but the ultimate questions such why does anything exist in the first place and what is it that enables us to be conscious of it all is still unanswerable. A *'technology'* which has been developed for countless eons of time is bound to be beyond our very primitive logic. It would appear that there are countless planes; worlds; and universes with vastly different natures perhaps even including places created by one's own mind. It seems we are back at square one where rather than being a product of the brain mind, and or the will, is the creator of all things.

So what do our spirit friends do when they are not working?

we have our own lives to look after, other friends, other loved ones, various projects helping out here and there, having our own pleasures and enjoyment: Taking in the sights and sounds of some of eternity's creations for there a myriad states of mind, places where everything is different, nothing is recognizable but which brings with it a wonderful insight, a wonderful release from the familiar and then the excitement of meeting these new conditions and bringing them home to think about to try to understand just as you are trying to understand us. So there are myriads of thought forms, of life, of places, of people everyone a part of our Father's mind that we may explore, that we may learn constantly, how our Father expresses Himself in so many different guises in so many different places. (6th August 2020)

What is it that directs the mind as if we are looking through a spy hole seeing and feeling our environment and being aware of our memory; making the decision to act; to choose; or not to choose. What power is it that we wield when we instruct the brain to do our bidding? With both hypnosis and the placebo effect there is a link between the mind and the brain which overrules the safety mechanism that uses pain to alert us to the danger of damage to our bodies from disease or for example touching something extremely hot. Hypnosis can radically change our senses and also the way we see the world. If mind and the body are separate entities why do individuals have to suffer so much terrible pain or overwhelming fear or pointlessness when there is theoretically an option to switch it off or even leave the body? (There are cases where this has happened spontaneously and also more commonly applies to some near-death experiences.)

The creation of all things is by the will of God. It is the impetus, the push if you like, the desire, the determination that precedes the force that sends the thought out and brings things to a conclusion. It reaches into the heart of the problem through reference to the memory which holds the experience of previous actions. Therefore the mind is tasked with looking into the memory, putting the pieces together and coming up with a conclusion and then when you are happy with that conclusion the will decides to run with it; to propose it; to make it happen and instructs the mind to carry out its tasks to follow that line of reasoning
The mind is a powerful instrument but not the be all and end all of life as you have put it, it is the carrier, of the

message, the envelope; the reaching out; the energy. The message has been created by the will, the awareness, the consciousness and this is the power of God as it seeks to explore the various strata of human consciousness, the different ideas and attitudes, the colour and the shape and the form of what is. (July & October 2019)

'Each soul as it inhabits the form brings evolution to the table. The human form has evolved over the timeline due to the soul adding elements to the experience. So the creation process involves the spiritual energy to contour the form to its individual needs for its own evolution.' ('*Veronica* 'April 2020.)

Even though learning to overcome the negative is part of the progressive or learning process I was surprised to discover that the fight between good and evil exists in the spirit world. According to astral travellers the earth's spirit world has a very strict moral structure. It is very definitely a place of levels between light and dark, darkness being the place where people have not yet progressed from brute ignorance. Selfish cruel people have created that state of mind and in the worst cases where they are gathered together they will torment each other rather like the violent inmates in some prisons until they have a change of mind which will bring them into brighter regions. Some who have addictions that they cannot satisfy prefer to remain close to the earth clinging to those of like minds from whom they can feel a second hand satisfaction and gain a certain amount of influence over their victims.

There are many minds that are opposed to our work they bring with them sadness, anger, bitterness. They like to win, they like to make the running and their mission is to discredit, to ruin, to harm, to deplete and to make a wreck out of people's lives. Then when they are satisfied, when they have burned out that bitterness then will come their regret, then they will see the error of their ways and they will come with glory and understanding and restitution; repairing the damage; guiding those who are without light;

leading them into calmer waters; showing them pitfalls and demonstrating the happiness which can result from a soul that has come home. Like the prodigal son, the blessed Father throws his arms around him and brings him into the light...(July 2020)

Judgement is automatic; the pattern of thoughts woven during a person's lifetime has taken them to that vibration. Sometime the conditions into which they were born might have contributed to being as they are. According to some near-death subjects at the moment of death immense kindness and understanding is shown to them even a choice as to which path to choose. There are mediums that run rescue circles for troubled souls brought by the *guides* to discuss their problems with members of the group. Some might be concerned with reaching out to a living person who maybe making life threatening decisions; others can't believe they have passed over. Ironically some who have been through the dark planes because of their experiences may be more advanced than someone who has never been tested. For the average person a spiritual home or a paradise garden has imperfections which reflect personal shortcomings.

The heaven I speak of is around about you now you cannot escape it, it is yours because you have made it even so and when the end comes you will see the beautiful garden but with blights, a few weeds, a difficult patch, a dull shaded, and cold..(June 2020)

This again is like our dreams where strange story lines reflect our waking experiences. According to *'Veronica'* how our lives could have turned out had we made different choices can be played out in spirit. (Issue 69 Inner Whispers Nov 20) Brightness is associated with highly advanced minds, to some mediums and those out of the body. Beings from the more advanced regions are dazzling in their brightness though quite ordinary in their own place. Some psychics claim to see our aura or halo which reflects the inner person, perhaps this inspired images from the ancient world which depict *'Saintly'* individuals said to have an extra brightness around the head.

I think we have a right to accept logic as our guide therefore I wonder would a world of mind be a chaotic place. Swedenborg wrote that whilst *'all things in heaven appear in place and in space exactly as they do in the world ... angels have no notion or idea of place and space.' He continued, 'This must of necessity appear paradoxical...' 'All changes of place in the spiritual world are affected by changes of the state of the interiors, so that a change of place is nothing else than change of state. ... Hence it is that they are near to each other who are in similar states, and distant who are in dissimilar states ... From this cause alone the heavens are distinct from one another, and also the societies of each heaven, and the individuals in each society. This is also the reason why the hells are entirely separated from the heavens, for they are in a contrary state.' 'One person becomes present to another provided only he intensely desires his presence...several who are in one place, see one another, so long as they agree, but as soon as they disagree, they disappear.'*

He wrote that when travelling from one place to another, *'he arrives sooner when he eagerly desires it and later when he does not.'*

(P120. 'Heaven and Hell.' Emanuel Swedenborg. 1689-1772. Swedenborg Society.)

'Albert Pauchard' says, *'where I am now, there are very few 'casual' meetings, such as happened in the beginning when I was much nearer earth. The laws of affinity and affection are much more evident ...' From two beings that attract each other there rises a wave of affection which lights their approachment with an intense light. That light takes various forms. Sometimes it resembles large wings, sometimes geometrical figures or flowers ... It is, so to speak, a gushing forth of luminous forms... an intense joy is created by such meetings - and this joy in itself is music.*

('The Other World.' P118. *'Albert Pauchard.'* Pelegrin Trust. 1952.)

What kind of an existence would it be without differences of opinion; discussion; disagreements? Surely a world where everyone was constantly happy without a variety of feelings wouldn't be a real world. Obviously the pressures of earth life are removed, there is a lightness that comes from not being in a heavy physical body and a feeling of well being however there will be serious issues to consider such as; how successful was the life you have just left; have you caused hurt that you feel guilty about; have you been able to manage your emotions such as anger; jealousy; revenge; impatience etc. No doubt there is the embarrassment or humiliation of being able to see and feel how other people have reacted to you. You will of course be affected as you see loved ones grieving and perhaps struggling on their own: Suddenly you have become a saint in their eyes on the other hand there are likely to be a myriad of kindnesses that you haven't even registered but I think also that the realisation that most of us suffer from the same faults will help enormously.

In our world we do have trials and tests of will; decision making; disappointments; sometimes a loss of direction but always we are able to overcome with the power that is within us given to us by our almighty Father and directed at our innermost soul, our innermost being. (August 2019)

Each plane, each realm, each district has something different to offer taking on some of the personality of the residents.

The spiritual worlds are in essence the epitome of all that is good and true. They are a reflection of that which is highest in man and his environment. We are in ourselves but a pale reflection of that which is of God. His message to us is one that is spiritual, which is an insight into causes, and effects that bring us knowledge of ourselves and the circumstances that surround us. In the spiritual world there are places which reflect each of these attributes: They are manifestations encompassing a certain outlook, a certain feeling, a certain train of thought, and these places are knitted together rather loosely and, as we progress, we journey from one level to another so that we can express ourselves in different regions. As we go we leave behind our miss-understandings and our misapprehensions and we follow onto something that is of a more enlightened state, a greater understanding. And so we progress slowly through the different regions until we arrive at a threshold, which is the beginning of a New World. In each of these places there are peculiarities, there are insights into what makes man what he is and what troubles him and these regions are tailor-made to cater for the very essence of the problem and of overcoming it. Each is a place of special endeavour to come to terms with that aspect of thinking, of living, with which it is concerned. As we move about our world we encounter each of these regions. We can take our time there and learn to come to terms with the things we are encountering and all in all there are always things to be learned; to be understood; to be taken account of and so whilst there are places there are also regions and worlds. As we gain understanding we leave behind those particular aspects which have troubled us and move onto something which is more generalised and at the end of the day we are charged with the mission to accelerate man's understanding by bringing him into the knowledge of what the journalists call, ('the peace that passeth all understanding.')

(Feb 1990 'The Spiritual Life 2016.' Michael Featherstone Amazon. UK)

The endeavours of those on this side of life to bring certain people into a new way of thinking are tremendous. Great thought is brought to bear sometimes and much ingenuity to achieve a certain end; to bring the soul back into the fold and into a fairer land for that is what we are talking about. The elevation that is reached, the thought patterns, are akin to certain planes, certain regions in our world and as we work with people so they change their affinity and become more in tune with the higher planes and with different regions of thought.

(August 1991. The Spiritual Life 2016. Michael Featherstone Amazon)

The other day I was watching TV and looking at amazing pictures of our own galaxy and beyond. There is no doubt that very heavy objects and even people can be moved about in séances by unknown forces but a universe! Those not privileged to witness such events can be forgiven for not believing them even knowing that nothing in the universe is truly solid. I can understand that the world has to be isolated from interference by any passing spirit therefore lifting a heavy piece of furniture or perhaps interfering with mechanical or electronic things could not be allowed under normal circumstances. The physical phenomena that we see is obviously created within the laws of this existence using emotional energy present in the environment including human beings some of whom have more than their fair share of it. To produce such a vast expanse like our universe perhaps there are a different set of laws and I can only wonder if it's an illusion. I'm trying hard to imagine the greater reality of which our universe is said to be a tiny part.:- Looking beyond our physical existence to the great beyond which it seems is an endless sea of mind with no beginning and no end it also would appear that our dreams have echoes of this reality. In dreams anything and everything is possible a dream can seem to be vividly real; time and distance are subjective. In communications from some mediums over the years we get a sense of normality in the afterlife places associated with earth where it is an idealised or a carbon copy of earth as if we take our memories with us: On the other hand there is a mixture, a blending of realities; Out-of-body travellers are aware of this ability to hallucinate and cannot always tell hallucination from reality. Mind can create in these worlds both unconsciously and consciously forming beautiful scenery and buildings to the satisfaction of the people there. There are rare hints of this phenomenon in our world bearing in mind that the physical universe is on a different vibration to the spiritual worlds. In view of the vast variety of forms in existence could the little people found in many cultures; fairies, pixies and gnomes be spirits or thought forms? There is a very well known case of a schoolmistress 'Emile Sagee.' At first there were reports of her being in two places at once. Subsequently the whole class frequently saw her double standing behind her copying every movement.

At one time she was picking flowers in the garden 'like one in a dream' whilst her double was sitting in an arm chair ... two of the girls' touched the apparition which seemed to offer a faint resistance like a piece of muslin or crepe. 'When asked 'if she had experienced any particular sensation ... she replied that she had merely reflected to herself on noticing the empty arm-chair that it was a matter for regret that the other mistress had gone off and left the class to their own devices, as she thought that would be wasting their time.' The whole thing caused such a stir that she was eventually asked to leave. She then went to live with her sister-in-law and her young children who became so used to her and her double that they often told people that they had two Aunt Emilies.

('The Mystery of the Human Double.'P67. Ralph Shirley. Olympia Press. 1972.)

'Alexandra David-Kneel, a French Buddhist, spent years learning the practices of Tibetan Yogis. Over a few months she built up a thought form of a short, stout, jovial lama which would perform actions that seemed to be independent from her. Her creation was mainly visual but sometimes she *'felt as if a robe was lightly touching (her) and once a hand seemed to touch (her) shoulder.'* She had seen such figures (tulpas) belonging to other people and a herdsman once saw her creation and took him to be a *'live lama'* (P284/285. 'With Mystics & Magicians in Tibet.' Penguin. 1931.)

There could yet be another part of us that can act as guide and mentor for throughout history there have been stories of Doubles or Doppelgangers warning of an impending accident or possible death. There are records of people being seen miles away from where they actually are and lots of reports that the body can continue doing quite intricate things whilst the consciousness looks on or is even

in another place. Dr Muller cites the case of the judge who saw his clerk's double come in and take a book off the shelf whilst the clerk himself was elsewhere telling a friend that if only he were able to look in that book he would get the information he wanted. (Excursions to the Spirit World' P136.)
Fredrick Sculthorpe was once listening to a lecture in spirit and was amazed to see his double listening intently in an adjacent chair. This he was told was his Higher Self. *'a healthy looking young man of about 23 with a full head of hair which* (he wrote) *in the physical body I lack.'*
(Fredrick Sculthorpe. P97. 'Excursions to the Spirit World.' Greater World. 1961.)

Brigitte Rix's book is a gripping and fascinating read it seems to take us back to square one almost to a kind of magical land certainly hard to visualise. Out of an infinite sea of *"creative energy force"* using mind and will power comes a desire to create, to progress. Our universe is but a tiny speck in infinity and was constructed by countless spirit beings. Whilst humans are made out of the same building blocks as other species the first spirits materialised their bodies to try out their creations until they were satisfied that they were fit for purpose.
('Worlds Beyond the Spirit World.' Brigitte Rix. CON-PSY Publication.
http://www.italkwithspirits.com/)

Is the following an example of a creation or simply a variation of the evolutionary process?
Palaeontologists started finding ancient humans, like H. naledi, (Star man) that are so strange, it is as if they had walked off the pages of a Tolkien fantasy. (300.000-200.000
(New scientist.How-ancient-proteins-are-untangling-humanitys-family-tree.
Colin Barras 2017)

And words from a *spirit* in a book published in 1909:-
'The germ of Immortal Life.' There must be a point...when 'I, myself' began as such to be.... In appearance it was separated and drawn from the grand reservoir but (became) .... a separate unit ...when dual forms of life in a certain state and sphere, and upon a certain occasion, received into their own forms an inflow of life, from a still

more interior and exalted state and within that inflow there
was something which within their forms became a unit.
('The Busy Life Beyond Death.'P6. John Lobb, F.R.G.S F.R. Hist.S. L.N. Fowler 1909.)

Although I have concluded that delving into religious texts and fabulous tales of heaven and hell would be even more confusing than enlightening I decided to have a quick look at Wikipedia and Google for ideas not as religious texts but for the echoes of what might be man's history. If there were some experimental human prototypes one of the sources for mankind's origins would be the first humans; stories passed down through the generations that were not simply made up imaginings or metaphors.

"....when the sons of God (The Nephilim.) came in unto the daughters of men, and they bare children to them, the same became mighty men which were of old, men of renown. (Possibly giants.) The first mention of the "sons of God" in the Hebrew Bible occurs at Genesis 6:1–4." As we are all technically sons of God that maybe misleading but there is a differentiation in the text.

Nobody knows who the Nephilim were. (Some translate as 'Fallen' angels.) Perhaps they were simply a different tribe. Could they be spirits testing out prototype bodies or were these merely fictional Gods that man has always believed in, were they space men or ordinary men; who knows?

Possibly the oldest civilisation are the Aborigines who believe in the world of the dead and that it blends with the real worlds. They also believe in reincarnation, and that various spirits were tasked with creating different aspects of our physical world
(answersingenesis.org/creationism/creation-myths/what-warlpiri-aborigines-believe-
about-origin-of-everything/ By Laurie Reece March 1986.)

The oldest signs of intelligence seem to be 1.8 million years ago in the shape of stone tools. Cave paintings on an Indonesian Island 44 thousand years old depicted humans with animal heads. No one knows what that could have meant possibly they were simply imaginary but there are similar reports of beings on the astral plane where dreamers and the earth bound meet: It is the ante room of the spiritual planes where there are thought forms, beings without a soul that use discarded astral bodies shed by animals and those that have moved on also powerful demonic beings formed out of the violent selfish addictive negative emotions of mankind.   ('Gone West. J.S.M.Ward.)

If the thought that some or all spirits skipped the evolutionary process and materialised rather than being born is hard to accept perhaps modifying the genes is more likely.   Here is part of a *'story'* written through Chico Xavier in trance:- '

People can actually help plan their own future bodies with the help of the genetic engineers at the Reincarnation Planning Department. Here, people waiting to be reborn for a specific purpose are able to ask for physical defects that will help them develop qualities they need. ... The physical laws of heredity are fully respected but now and then 'modifications can be impressed on matter', such as a bad leg, a weak heart or more serious disabilities.
(P150. 'The Indefinite Boundary.' Guy Lyon Playfair. Panther. 1976.)

The big question is, if the future can be seen how do we explain the despot who will cause so much pain and sorrow to countless others?   Is he aware of the journey he was about to embark upon? I can only assume that cause and effect trumps all other considerations.

The spirit world is the author of life, every stick and stone must be thought about every creature activated, all animals brought under the umbrella of God's children, God's creation however small however tiny. And they all have one thing in common they are fundamentally spirit beings each on its own pathway; intermingling; interacting; learning from each other; learning to forgive; learning to care; and learning to do what they can for their fellow spirits and this wonderful world which has been loving crafted: No stone unturned in its creation and nothing left to chance remember that. (February 2020)

If all beings were designed by influencing the evolutionary process maybe one day we will meet the designers of earth's wonderful creations; the birds; the animals; the creatures of the sea, the human body and even the tiny bugs which are an essential part of the ecosystem; all of them have the qualities of design; of inventiveness; of artistry. The nearest phenomenon that might link mind with physical creation is when a ghost appears to be indistinguishable from a human being. Elizabeth Kubler Ross recalled seeing a lady whom she knew to be dead, getting out of a lift. To assure herself that she wasn't imagining this she got her to write a note. This is the nearest we will get to whether the biblical stories of angels interacting with men were real or imagined. There are sources which claim that in the beginning humans had the ability to pop in and out of the body at will. During her out-of-body excursions Rosalind McKnight was told that *Angels can appear on earth temporarily* (in) *human form to perform miracles.* (P113. Soul Journeys. Hampton Roads. 2005.)

Just to complicate matters not everyone sees the same thing it seems to be a matter of tuning in as is obvious when a medium is describing a person in the room that no one else can see: Perhaps this is in the mind of the medium or it is a real spirit person in the room. At other times people see someone that appears to be real in time and space only once in their life. There are quite a few books on the subject of angels, in some instances a figure appears in full daylight, has the power to lift objects, saves the day and is _seen_ to disappear. The mechanism is obviously there and under some control however mediums have to spend years developing the power for spirits to materialise. Whilst the 'dead' probably appear to their families far more often than is generally known one might imagine that if spirits could influence physical matter so easily there would be chaotic consequences. As it is their unseen *influence* is probably more common than we might like to believe. That entirely newly designed and created fully-developed bodies might have been used in the beginning is interesting as a baby knows nothing whilst an adult would presumably bring with it some experience and awareness of the spirit world. The following story highlights the countless heart-breaking occasions when we would wish that something or someone would save the day but doesn't. If Angels were once human beings they won't always be dressed in white! -What are we to make of the story of a lady who was being mugged when a punk came from behind and knocked the mugger to the ground.

'The youth'... 'dressed in a black studded leather jacket and trousers' ... (with) *a ' bright pink Mohican hairstyle which stood on end about six inches into blue spikes'... 'gave her' the most dazzling smile'* ... *'and vanished in front of 'her eyes!'* ('Mystic Forces'. P214. Peter & Mary Harrison. Sinclair. 1989)

There are many occasions during physical séance's where matter is manipulated in the most amazing ways.

The Union of Spiritualist Mediums' president Eileen Roberts described a séance at Stansted Hall Essex with Gordon Higginson in trance. *'ectoplasm was emerging from his nose and mouth. When invisible hands rolled up his jumper ectoplasm was seen coming from his solar plexus.'* Throughout this Gordon seemed quite comfortable. '... *it became obvious that there was a step-by-step control of the ectoplasm as it flowed copiously, was quickly removed or when it took definite shape or form. Each step was announced by the spirit voices beforehand. ...the ectoplasm, sometimes yards in length, was propelled forward over the floor like someone shaking out folds of material. Occasionally it seemed like gossamer web with thick draperies on each side of a fine veil... From being transparent it became shaped and hung in folds down the medium's trunk. These folds then changed into a seeming liquid appearance soft and silken to the touch. Gradually they twisted and turned into a rope-like structure. Then the change continued into a smoother substance. Next it became a long square-sided rod with the ridges vanishing. What finally emerged was a smooth rod with such solidity that heavy physical pressure could not move or bend it.'*

Then 'it was announced that the next demonstration would be "how we make the mould" for spirit forms to become visible. Gordon's left hand and arm were lifted gently to shoulder height. The clearly visible ectoplasm coming from nose and mouth formed into heavy folds along the arm's upper surface, increasing in amount over the back of his hand. A spirit voice... invited Eileen to place her hand over this small pudding shape. This was perfectly folding into itself like thick cream on pudding. All the time the structure was changing the soft, slightly crunchy texture became firm like an orange that could be squeezed then it grew harder like a snowball. Finally it became a solid ball which resisted all her pressure and could not be physically dented. At this stage, says Eileen came the experience that had a profound effect on her. Between the medium and the ectoplasmic ball there was obviously the presence of an intelligent mind concentrating on controlling the ectoplasm, making it change its structure. The changes happened under her hands as she pushed and squeezed as requested.'
(Then) … 'forms materialised giving correct information about identity and evidence of survival. This was accompanied by a request to speak to sitters who were named. ... (After which came)...'the announcement ... that a guide would materialise in front of Gordon and disappear though the floor. This female guide's voice was heard coming from beneath the floor as she said she would repeat her demonstration. This time she rose through the floor and laughed as she showed her materialisation again. It was, Eileen rightly says, a superb example of spirit intelligence at work demonstrating a supreme knowledge of chemistry and energy manipulation.' (Psychic News.)

According to Brigitte Rix's mum *"if one activates something from here it can become real in your world!*

.......If one sends strong thoughts it makes them appear on earth ". (P250,I'm not dead I'm Alive. Brigitte Rix Con-Psy 2011)

The universe may only be huge in terms of a human being perhaps the physicist, Sir Arthur Eddington FRS was right when he said, *'The stuff of the world is mind stuff.'*

(The Nature of the Physical World. MacMillan 1928.)

The particles which make up the fabric of our universe vibrate at higher rates in the spirit world which it seems makes them more malleable and more responsive to the power of the mind. Turning to the greater reality that includes our almost miniscule universe in the great scheme of eternity could it be a force field, a system that allows mind to create upon it; to visualise; to sculpt it; coupled with a great memory from which images can appear at will. Perhaps this is the source of our dreams morphed with real memories as we assess and try to come to terms with our problems and experiences. Someone I was told understood these concepts whilst out-of-body but like a forgotten dream were lost and he was in tears that he had to return.

Thought is a wonderful thing. It has been created by the Father as an instrument, a means of expression and also a means of projecting power that is in itself intelligent it has all the qualities of the human mind and more besides. It knows the direction of travel, it can pick up on the slightest inference, it is the fundamental process by which the universe works but your attempts to delimitate it to bring it into the human perspective will not appease the sceptics will not help really in any way save to pose the question and as we cannot see round corners and do not understand the basics of the spiritual processes, it is in fact a lost cause. (December 2020)

Astronomers say they have spotted an intriguing link between galaxies separated by large distances, pointing to the existence of a vast structure underlying the universe known as the cosmic web. (New Scientist 2019)

'Veronica' was asked 'Does the nonlinear and outer space have any correlation?' 'The nonlinear is a vast arena of fluidity. It is not a backdrop for planetary paths. The energy in nonlinear is an easy canvas for creation. Outer space is a tableau of support for the movement within its parameters. It only looks endless from your point of view.'

('*Veronica*' through April Crawford 'Inner Whispers' Jan 2020.)

'...the spirit world is unknowable until you have been or seen and experienced and thought and explored.' (Jan 2020)

Continuing with the idea that everything could be an illusion in terms that time and space did not really exist:-

Some... posit that, in Buddhism the perceived reality is considered illusory not in the sense that reality is a fantasy or unreal, but that our perceptions and preconditions mislead us to believe that we are separate from the elements that we are made of. Reality, in Buddhist thought, would be described as the manifestation of **karma**.

As a prominent contemporary **Buddhist** *teacher puts it: "In a real sense, all the visions that we see in our lifetime are like a big dream ...In this context, the term 'visions' denotes not only visual perceptions, but appearances perceived through all senses, including sounds, smells, tastes and tactile sensations, and operations on received mental objects.* (Wikipedia)

During Robert Monroe's adventures out of the body he has been able to meet with the beings of light and hear about something of their reality. Individuals, yet part of a whole, they claim that their *'ability and knowledge seem without limit yet we know at this point such is valid only within the energy systems of our experience. We can create time as we wish or the need arises, reshaping and modifying within the precept itself. We can create matter from other energy patterns, or change the structure thereof to any degree desired ... We can create, enhance, alter, modulate, or eradicate any precept within the energy fields of our experience ... We cannot create or comprehend our prime energy until we are complete. We can create physical patterns such as your sun and solar system, yet we do not. It has been done. We can adjust the environs of your planet Earth, yet we do not. It is not our design.' 'We can and do monitor, supplement, and enhance the flow of human learning experience, as well as other learning experiences of similar content throughout time-space. This we perform continuously at all levels of awareness so as to prepare properly those entraining units of our prime energy for the entry and meld into the totality that we are becoming.* '(P122)

The being of light speaks of *'Energy systems'-'energy fields'-'prime energy'* Monroe states that (I was) *'... astounded that I remained as calm as I had in the face of the encounter that was taking place ... the effrontery of my probing, the extent of my ignorance ... Their radiant response to these flickers of thought was so profound that I nearly broke down and lost control, no patronising, no compassion, no feeling of superiority ... but beyond friendship, beyond brotherhood, beyond father- mother- parent, beyond endearment, beyond words ... If they had told me they were my God-creator, I would have settled for that.'* (And in reply to that last thought came the response.) *'But we are not, Mister Monroe.'* (P102.) Asked about their destination they replied:- *'We believe it to be the source of radiation, the creative emission and return. Communication is closed with those who have continued. The desire to continue occurs upon completion.*

(P123. 'Far Journeys.' Robert A. Monroe. Doubleday. 1985.)

After abandoning mediumship for years of research into clairvoyance Eileen Garrett concluded that the subconscious mind was able to reach out to all *'possible realms of understanding...'* Colin Wilson calls this *'a recognition that we are living in an information universe and that all this information is accessible to certain levels of the human mind.'*

(P298. Beyond The Occult. Colin Wilson. Guild Publishing. 1988.)

In the true spiritual planes there are things that are beyond description, which need to be experienced to be understood. There is an all pervading atmosphere which will take over the very being, which is the individual, to such an extent that it becomes a part of him and is in essence the accumulative personality, accumulative product of the expressions of many lives and as such is more powerful because of its great wisdom and experience.

(Nov. 1990. The Spiritual Life 2016 - Michael Featherstone.)

'THE PLANE OF WHITE LIGHT.' The sixth plane.'

Here the spirit bears, 'the incalculable secret wisdom ... garnered from lives passed in myriad forms.' They are capable of living without form, of existing as white light, as the pure thought of their Creator. They have joined the immortals.' (P71. 'F.W.H Myers.' 'The Road to Immortality.' Geraldine Cummins.)

When finally the planes are reached which require no physical expression there is a deep rapport with the other inhabitants who live in a state of animated thought. It is still true to say that things represent those thoughts for they are the means by which these finer feelings have been experienced have been built up but in their own way these thoughts are purely an expression of something spiritual. When there is complete absorption into the God-Head the things which have created these states of mind are but shadows and the new experience is far beyond our capacity to explain. (15.8.91) (P38 'The Spiritual Life' Michael Featherstone. Amazon.)

In the spiritual world there are so many dimensions, so many aspects to living which have not been explored that we cannot possibly say what is beyond the reach of our own experience. There are planes that have never been visited from this level. In essence they are behind closed doors and yet something of their character rains down upon us. It is as if all heaven was opened up to this glorious power of love.- (3ʳᵈ Oct. 1991) (P38.The Spiritual Life 2016 Michael Featherstone.)

'OUT YONDER, TIMELESSNESS. 'The seventh plane.
'Though formless,' ...the soul is...'in contact with the whole of the material universe; an incredible activity of a spiritual and intellectual kind is theirs. For now they share in the timeless Mystery; ... they know and experience the alpha and omega of the material universe. ... (P52.) You are as you climb the long ladder of consciousness, a sum in arithmetic. When you pass out yonder you become the whole. The spirit which lights up the ladder is an individualised thought of God.' (P53.) You, as part of the Whole-and by the Whole I indicate God-may be likened to the sun; your rays pervade the material universe, yet your spirit remains detached from it, reigning in the great calm of eternity. (P73.)
('The Road to Immortality.' *'FWH Myers.* 'Geraldine Cummins. Psychic Press Ltd. 1932.)

Mankind's dream of an afterlife turns out to be a reality but the reality of the afterlife would seem to be contained within a dream or some highly complex programming of which mankind can never learn. Our God is not a bearded old man in the sky but a vast consciousness in which we all share. Whilst there are those who are un-progressed and have the same freewill sometimes to wreak havoc in the world the greater part of that consciousness has within it a formidable active force for good and at its pinnacle, perfection; presumably the source of all that is. These advance souls must surely have the capacity to calculate and to access vast amounts of data and memories. Each and every one of us lowly human beings is in essence a spirit with a connection to the God within which in itself is part of the God without. Then there are the Helpers and or the Guides, which are described by that inspiring word, 'Angels'; the ancient name for messenger. These are individuals like you and I, though surely far more advanced, working constantly for the good of each one of us; the group that we one day may want to join as we oversee our loved ones to keep them on the right track. Do they have magic wands and perform miracles? One may call the work they do miraculous, who knows, it seems that they use logic, experience and hard work to persuade; to inspire and to try to engineer certain outcomes always conscious of man's free will and the life plan decided on before birth.

..and to put before the bar of man the chance to open up the gates of knowledge; to understand the greater reality; to make him think yes, to allow him to see new visions of what life really is rather than the vague woolly notions which brings heaven down to a playground; a never, never land; unreal; not challenging; a fool's paradise; a place where the imagination reigns; not real; not welcoming even. (May 2020.)

I remember an address by Most Rev Lyn Gibb-deSwarte who once said the 'dead' were more alive than the congregation she was talking to. (Probably containing quite a few who were bereaved.) They are full of fun and enthusiasm, they know that you might not have had the opportunity to say goodbye and that you loved them; they have seen the new baby, they share in your news good and bad.

Although I can accept the reason for tragedy I still find it hard when I see the terrible things that happen to people and animals. I think spirits who take part in these dramas must be strong minded to say the least and yet the Second World War for example, hell-like though it was for many, has given us some thoroughly absorbing stories of bravery and valour, inventiveness and progress. For many both world wars brought a leap forward, the slave / master situation was diminishing and more equality was to follow. Nature too seems to exist through violence, an essential way to assure survival of the fittest as part of a highly complicated ecosystem.

Some of R.J. Lees' characters were immensely proud of the suffering that they had gone through in their lives. The fact is if there was no such thing as mountains those with a sense of adventure and of looking danger in the face, would invent them.

...the truth is that spirit is real, life is wonderful and is not intended to debilitate or grind people down but to bring them up to a higher standard, more optimistic, easier to handle life because of their experiences and someone to whom people can

turn in a crisis: The getting together as friends as we inhabit and experience this world with all of its glories and all of its pain and suffering which in turn will bring us to a higher point in the spirit world than if we had not been here at all. There would be no point in having soldiers if they did not go through rigorous training. (February 2020)

In times past men looked to nature and events for signs and portents to try to read the mind of God for example if a battle was won then God had obviously willed it so. We can now appreciate such ideas as primitive, futile but even so, perhaps with hindsight, we might feel that something, call it *'fate,'* changed the course of our lives. The phrase that I was impressed with was *'God is everywhere always working...'* Considering the God within and countless numbers of Guides and helpers it would appear that human beings are like goldfish in bowl; we are an open book, a daunting thought, comforting to some; embarrassing even frightening to others. One wonders how much influence is brought to bear in the world of man particularly from the higher levels considering the life plan, free will and the possibility that awful things might have been avoided. Apparently where a difficult event cannot be changed there is tremendous support given by the helpers and as they say you will get your rewards in heaven.

Our family is much bigger than we could ever imagine, Mums, Dads, Sons, Daughters, Brothers, Sisters, friends and colleagues, brothers in arms from other lives helping, following our progress, with that invisible bond of love which has continued throughout the centuries.

Some races are privy to our work but they expect too much rather than a partnership there is the expectation that we command all events and determine their outcome Now whilst we may see the results of what is going on we in no way create that situation other than to try to ameliorate, to support and guide and prevent people from taking things too badly. All in all being a sympathetic ear and holding back whatever forces we can to ease the burden to sooth the troubled mind. (July 2020.)

Our history is filled with legends, dramas and beliefs of the most improbable kind because we are like the man in the car factory who has no knowledge of technology, applied research and logic. In reality it seems that we *are* the technology, in dreams and in spirit our higher mind can shape and mould and create its own environment sometimes shared sometimes solitary. Like human beings it wants to achieve, explore and learn new things on its journey to the ultimate; overcoming our own lesser selves and that of others without which the world would have less challenges and less opportunity to progress.

We want to help you as far as we can with your book but reality is a knotty problem there are never going to be ample explanations which will satisfy the most critical minds. There will always be an opt-out clause, disbelief, discouragement; dismay. Leave it alone they will say it's not worth the candle it's not worth pursuing. When the time comes for these things to be revealed it will be a long, long way into the future when man has taken many twists and turns in his adventures: When knowledge has increased so much so that things never thought possible will become real and then will the attitude and the viewpoint of the many change as they see the results of agonising; researching; probing; peering into the abyss; into the thoughts and ideas of the visionaries who were always one jump ahead but never really get any credit for it for they were ahead of their time. When we give somebody our point of view; our knowledge; our impression there is always the caveat that what is given is accepted in the correct manner for when tales are told they are invariably altered in the telling. The emphasis may be different the words also therefore things are rarely pure so that when we tell how it is you may put your own spin on it because of your attitude; your beliefs; your outlook; your preference for certain ideas. (July 2019)

We know that you have sometimes gone around in circles and that you would wish to have a clearer picture of the ultimate reality however we have explained that this is not a concept that you can readily grasp from the human point of view. The efforts that you have made in that direction will serve you well and will at least indicate the difference between human reality and spiritual realities for there is an element of truth in what you are thinking, what you have concluded. It is a vastly more complicated subject than you could ever imagine and as you have readily understood that time being of no barrier has brought all these things into being; layer upon layer; second upon second; year upon year: Minds beavering away; experiences; mistakes; misunderstandings all added to the mix to bring about the reality which is of spirit; of the power of the Almighty; the regions above which oversee which calculate which concern themselves with the perfect running of everything that is. In the minds of those who are far above us there are visions beyond belief in another sphere of activity and that is what we are aiming for: Calculating; working hard; dealing with the negative; excited at the positive coming to conclusions; all of these wonderful things; adventures; successes; delays; and deliberations; disappointments and then breakthroughs. We are all of us very busy people; seeking to understand; to grow; to conquer; to have an experience never-to-be forgotten and to roll out the red carpet as we take our place on the thought pattern which leads to God: Elevating our souls, and bringing with us those weaker than ourselves, those in need of our experience, those to whom we can relate; appeal; concentrate; coming with us on the journey as we light the way as we reach out to the higher realms and we look down at those on the road following us in our light delighting in their new-found freedom and understanding, coming to us as we beckon them on, as we lead the way.(2019)

Finally thoughts from my friend and colleague '*Frank*', with whom I have had countless discussions and referring to my habit of retreating into the gloom.

It's different over here; you and me would never have understood the reality of it, I have great difficulty even now getting my head around it. Don't come in a state of mind that will hold you back it's not necessary. Buck Up! There are scenes of wonder; of delight; curiosity; and weird: Full of life they intrude into your mind if you let them. Come to us in a happy frame of mind. (2019.)

This book *is a work of thoughtfulness, accuracy, and lovingly crafted by those who have inspired you over the years and added to your efforts with their wisdom and their knowledge of the subject from the point of view of human beings. From our view it is a very different thing which cannot be put into human terms but which can only deal in metaphors, similarities and, vague shadows: Yes it is disappointing that it cannot ever be a clear and structural text book of reality. The effort which has gone in has shaped and moulded the text so that the reader can identify, can believe, can accept, can know of the world of spirit and that should suffice. Those who want to go a little deeper can themselves look for evidence and see what they might see, understand what they might understand but they too will find a limitation to what can be understood. The work is the result of many years of pondering, thinking, arguing, looking and considering and even now you have your thoughts upon what is quite right and what is wide of the mark but it will all become clear one day.* (January 2020.)

There are still things which appear to me to be contradictory and food for more thought. It is apparent that we are never going to comprehend the 'technology' of our material universe or indeed the greater reality which has been evolved over an unimaginable length of time by an infinite number of minds. Suffice to say that reality is far, far and away more complex and wonderful that any human mind can comprehend. To sum it all up in more words from Douglas Adams,

'*It is a mistake to think you can solve any major problems just with potatoes*' (Hitchhiker's Guide to the Galaxy. Douglas Adams.)

Then when I thought the book was complete this came:-

The universe is in a different realm a place where only spirit is the reality. Things of earth are in a different dimension, not so tangible to us as you would think. Leave behind the world of man and come with us into the world of spirit. In our world we

are creating constantly. It is part of the fabric of the spirit world so nothing in your dimension comes as a surprise to us because it is in the natural order of things that thoughts bring about tangible and real events, scenery, objects, people even. The malleable atmosphere of existence, of creation allows us to paint pictures, to create objects, to have vistas as wide as your universe because these things take no space, no time, no place, they just are. And that is what you are going to discover. The features of this world are constructed by mind, through will, through determination, through visualization and when it is created the spirit that dwells there dwells within that creation, is related to it, is relevant to it. The ego decides, the ego is all, the impressions that you make on the ether construct, take shape and reach the eye of the beholder as a solid object, a place to go, somewhere to be seen, or an avenue of thought, suspended in eternity, not taking up any space or time but being there where we put it. Then when it is no longer required, it fades away, it evaporates and so it is with your world. When the universe grows old we shall see the change, the metamorphosis, as human beings return gradually to spirit and the universe will fade and die and in its place will come new thoughts, new zones, new ideas, and new activities: All dreamt up by those who wish to inhabit, to explore, to experience. That universe may be very different from the present one and the spirits who go there will be the spirits who have always been there ready to see anew, do something different, create, mould, build, experience, conquer, and then when that period is over there will be another, and another, and another: People, places phases, ideas, constructs in a never-ending chain. Love in abundance conquering all, always looking out on a new and exciting horizon, a new challenge, refreshing, anticipating something new, something good. Leave behind the serious, the crestfallen, the doubt, the down hearted. Look into the face of goodness, of love, of positivity, achievement: Something which will bring you joy and returns for all your hopes and wishes and kind thoughts.

(Feb 2020) .

Has my amble through the various facts and speculation given you food for thought or are you still unconvinced? Confused perhaps! This is not a text book, we do not know how advanced the communicators are or how pure the channel is between *them* and the medium. It would however be good if I have shown that life after death is at least feasible.

We are the Scientists; the Philosophers; the teachers; the Pupils; the Parent; the Child; and the Creators: It is our universe and we are aspects of God though in our present state far from perfection. It's like working for a business and feeling like an insignificant cog in the machine, a victim of circumstance but in reality we are an essential part of the team, our presence influences those around us and when we are gone we leave behind us an empty space because we have shared in the lives of others. We are part of everything that is and everything that is, is a part of us, all that we experience has value even including the blackest moments. I think that the most profound thing that I can say is that we chose our present life for a reason; something we wanted to experience; someone we wanted to be with or help; something we wanted to know, understand or learn to overcome. There is a plan and we are living it and no one is alone or lost in this great adventure that we call life.

The single aim is that the reader shall accept the reality of spirit which has its implications for life eternal, fulfilment, happiness, purpose, a reason to get up in the morning and an acceptance of all of us in the family of God. (December 2019.)

When we teach you we want you to understand this; that they are but sketches; outlines; proposals; ideas; dreams even: Intended to fill that void in your mind; in the mind of man that sees a dead end, no light at the end of the tunnel; nothing to hope for; an existence which is bleak and threatening and we want you to emphasize that where mankind goes many have been before. Hope is eternal, there is no life save this one; no beginning; no end, no middle, it just is. Suspended in eternity as we are, we are but a droplet in a sea and yet we are the sea. Our presence is seen by the whole of creation, and yet we see it not. The purpose for which you were born was to enlighten, to bring thoughtful ideas to people so that they can move on; perhaps grab a little hope, the prospect of something which does not tell of annihilation but which is optimistic. A magical world it may appear to be but then so is the world you are living in now. In time we will see between the primitive and the technical and so it is on a sliding scale. Mankind will one day gain momentum, more understanding and look back upon these days as being primitive. (Feb 2020)

A small china tea pot orbiting the sun and a creator which is a flying spaghetti monster are scenarios used as putdowns of creationalism by Bertrand Russell and Bobby Henderson who no doubt were imaging God creating the universe with a wave of his magic wand. Even for the open minded the hard reality of this existence tends to eclipse the idea of the universe being created. Whatever that might mean in practice like our day to day reality it's sure to be a highly logical and complex process, a technology evolved over an eternity. All we can do is remember how strange it is that we exist at all. I recall the words that came into my head as I left mam's empty flat after her death;

Row, Row, Row your boat gently down the stream,
merrily, merrily, merrily, merrily life is but a dream.

Mike Featherstone 2021

THE RESEARCHERS.

Air Chief Marshal Lord Dowding
1st Baron Dowding, GCB, GCVO, CMG
Alfred Russell Wallace OM FRS.
Professor Archie Roy. Emeritus Professor of Astronomy, University of Glasgow (1924-D 2012.)
Brian Inglis. journalist, historian television presenter. (1916 1993)
Carl G Jung. Psychiatrist psychoanalyst
Prof Bernard Carr. Maths/Astronomy
Colin Wilson. Author
Dr Charles Tart
Dr Ian Currie Author.(1936-1992)
Dr R.L.Morris Psychologist, Parapsychologist
Dr Karlis Osis. Ph.D.
Erlendur Haraldsson, Ph.D.
Dr Peter Fenwick Neuropsychiatrist **& Elizabeth Fenwick.**
Dr Wilson Van Dusen
Dr. Lyall Watson. Botanist, zoologist, biologist,
Dr. Maurice Rawlings.
Edmund Gurney. Psychologist
Frank Podmore. Parapsychologist/Sceptic.
Fredrick Myers. (1843–1901), Fellow of Trinity College, Cambridge; Classicist and Philosopher
Prof.Gary E. Schwartz, psychologist, author professor at the University of Arizona and the Director of its Laboratory for Advances in Consciousness and Health
Dr Ivor Grattan Guinness,
Prof Crawford.
Hannen Swaffer. Journalist and drama critic.
Pierre & Marie Curie.
Professor Henry Sidgwick., Trinity College, Cambridge; Philosopher Economist
F. C. S. Schiller (1864–1937), Fellow, Corpus Christi College, Oxford; Philosopher
Eleanor Sidgwick (1845–1936), Principal, Newnham College, Cambridge; Physicist
John Logie Baird, Invented TV.
Keith Harary. Parapsychologist
Kenneth Ring and Sharon Cooper

Sir Lawrence Evelyn Jones
(1885–1955) Honorary Fellow, Balliol College, Oxford; Author
Dr Marylyn Schlitz PhD. IONS Senior Fellow, Social Anthropologist.
Dr Bernard Haisch.
Dr Theo Locher
Dr Andreas Liptay-Wagner
Dr Paul Kurthy
Dr Ingrid Slack Psychologist Open University.
Dr Ernst Senkowski
Dr Hans-Peter Schaer Lawyer SPR
Dr Kurt Hofman
Dr Ulf Israelson
Dr Hans Peter Studer
Dr Maurice Rawlings MD.
Maurice Barbanell,
Journalist. Publisher, Psychic Press Ltd Medium for' *Silver Birch.* '
Montague Keen Journalist –
Eleanor & Henry Sidgewick.
James Webster. Surgical Chiropodist & Podiatrist.X member of magic circle
Raymond Moody MD
Reverend Stainton Moses,
Gerald Balfour (1853–1945), Politician, Fellow of Trinity College, Cambridge
Professor Gilbert Murray (1866–1957),
Regius Professor of Greek, University of Oxford.
Henry Arthur Smith (1848–1922), Barrister-at-Law, Middle Temple, London; Lawyer and author of legal treatises
Andrew Lang (1844–1912),
Fellow, Merton College, Oxford; Classicist and writer on folklore, mythology, and religion
William Boyd Carpenter
KCVO (1841–1918), Pastoral Lecturer,
Cavendish Professor John William Strutt, 3rd Baron Rayleigh OM, PRS (1842–1919), Trinity College, Cambridge; Physicist, Nobel Prize, Physics 1904 Theology, Cambridge; Bishop of Ripon
Sir William Barrett FRS.
Melvin Morse MD

Michael Bentine
PhD Dr Keith Hearne.
Physicist Russell Targ
Prof Ian Stephenson.
Prof John Hasted
Prof Raudive
Prof. J.H.Hyslop. Columbia University.
Professor John Beloff.
Steve Parsons
Professor Charles Richet. (1850–1935)
Nobel Prize in Medicine/Physiology 1913
Professor Ellison,
Professor Stewart Balfour
Owenham College, Manchester; Physicist
Arthur Balfour (1848–1930) Prime Minister
Sir Alister Hardy (1896–1985), Zoologist
Samuel Soal (1889–1975). Mathematician
Gilbert Murray (1915)
F. J. M. Stratton (1881–1960),
Astrophysicist, Professor in Cambridge University
Guy William Lambert (1889–1984), Diplc
Professor E. R. Dodds (1893–1979),
Hellenist, Birmingham and Oxford
George Nugent Merle Tyrrell
(1879–1952), Mathematician physicist, radio eng
William Henry Salter (1880–1969), Lawyc
Gardner Murphy (1895–1979),
Director of Research, Menninger Foundation,
Topeka, Kansas; Psychologist
John George Piddington (1869–1952),
Businessman, John George Smith & Co., London
Edith Lyttelton (born as Edith Balfour;
1865–1948), Writer
C. D. Broad (1887–1971), Philosopher
Robert Strutt, 4th Baron Rayleigh
(1875–1947), Physicist
H. H. Price (1899–1984), Philosopher
Robert Henry Thouless (1894–1984),
Psychologist
Hereward Carrington ASPR
Dr Rupert Sheldrake biochemist,
parapsychologist.
Prof Albert Einstein.
Prof Max Plank
George Meek.
Dr Dean Radin University of Nevada

Professor William McDougall FRS
(1871–1938), Duke University; Psychologist,
founder J B Rhine Parapsychology Lab
Walter Franklin Prince
(1863–1934) Clergyman
Elisabeth Kübler-Ross, Psychiatrist.
Prof. Camille Flammarion (1842–1925),
founder and first president of the Société
Astronomique de France, author of
popular science .
Professor Hans Driesch
(1867–1941) Universitaet Leipzig;
German Biologist and Natural
Philosopher, performed first animal
cloning 1885
Prof. Adrian Parker
Henri Bergson (1859–1941) Professor,
Collège de France, Paris; Chair of Modern
Philosophy;
Nobel Prize, Literature 1927 Thomas
Walker Mitchell (1869–1944), Physician
and Psychologist,
William James. ASPR
James Hewat McKenzie parapsychologist,
founder British College of Psychic Science.
1869-1929
William Thomas Stead Editor. 1849-1912-
Arthur Findlay MBE JP 1883 –1964
Founder Spiritualist College at Stansted Hall
Schrenck-Notzing 1862 – 1929 physician,
psychiatrist and notable psychical researcher.
Professor Donald West ,
Dr Hans Schaer. Lawyer
Alexander Graham Bell Professor.
Walter Franklin Prince ASPR
Maurice Grosse SPR
Victor Zammit retired attorney
Professor Alan Gauld, MA, DLitt, PhD,
Professor David Fontana. psychologist,
parapsychologist
Prof. Brian Josephson, Nobel prize-
winning physicist from Cambridge University
Prof. Jan Vandersande.
Pro David Bohm
J.J.Thompson.
Glen Hamilton
Prof.Haraldson

***There are many more author/researchers and mediums some of
which are included in this volume.

BIBLIOGRAPHY

IN THE BEGINING.

Stephen Hawking. Quote 'The Universe'.. P5
'Squealing plants' New Scientist. 2019.. P7
Intelligent Spiders. 'New Scientist.' Feb 2020... P7
Hoyle / Wickramsinghe. 'Evolution from Space.' Dent. 1991....................... P12

BEINGS OF LIGHT

In Our Time, BBC Radio 4. 22nd Sept 2016.. P16
'Start the Week.' BBC Radio 4. May 96.. P16
Physicist Vlatko Vedral. New scientist May 2020.. P17

POINTS OF VIEW

Telegraph... P21
'The Time and the Place' ITV.. P22

THE FRAGMENTED SELF

'Manipulation.' Erwin Laush. Fontana. 1972... P28
'Afterlife.' Colin Wilson. Harrap. 1985... P28
'Brain Story.' Prof. Susan Greenfield. BBC2. 1-8 2,000.............................. P30
Prof. V.S.Ramachandran. 'Phantoms in the Brain.' Channel 4' June 2,000.... P31
Brain rewires Independent.. P31

REALITY AND ILLUSION

Van Gogh Quote P33
Schapell conjoined sisters... P33

ARTIFICIAL INTELLIGENCE

Neurons in lockdown. Stanford University. New Scientist May 2020............. P37
The 'Conversation Newsletter' Jonathan Este. Nov 2022.............................. P37
Kevin Warwick P12. 'The Observer Magazine.' 17th Oct. 1993..................... P37

MEMORY

Shirichefski – Memory 'BBC Radio 4.' 9th August 2001............................. P38
The Boy who could remember everything Channel 4..................................... P38
Lifetide. Lyall Watson.. P38
Kim Peek. (Memory) Sunday Telegraph' Magazine. 23rd Jan. 2005............. P39
Flo & Kay Leman (Memory)... P39
Paul McKenna (Memory)... P39
Wilder Penfield'Closer to The Light.' Morse - Perry. Bantam Books. 1991... P40
Loss of Memory UK Living... P40
Loss of Memory 'The Unexplained. Robert Stack. Sky One. 1994................. P40

HYPNOSIS

Hypnosis Paul McKenna.. P42
Hypnosis P2182. 'The Unexplained.' Orbis.. P42
'Human Personality....' by FWH Myers "Longmans." 1907 Journal of SPR.. P43
'Beyond The Occult' P64. Guild Publishing. 1988.. P43

ABC Science. Professor Kristie Miller. University of Sydney 2028............................ P61
Michael Bentine 'The Door Marked Summer.' Granada. 1981............................... P62
Eddie Slasher 'Explorations Out of the Body.' P108. Kroshka Books 1997.................... P62
Precognition. John Godley............................ P62
Eddie Slasher 'Explorations out of the body'. P119 Kroshka. Books 1997.................... P62
Russell Targ, Keith Harari' Stanford Research. Horizon.' BBC.TV. 1983...................... P63
Prof Ian Stephenson. Reincarnation............................ P63
'The Man Who Dreamed the Future.' Channel 5. 10th September 2007........................... P63
'Life Before Life.' Helen Wambach. Bantam Books. 1979............................ P64
'The Paranormal.' P80. Brian Inglis. Paladin 1985............................. P66
Albert Einstein Precognition............................ P66

BEYOND THE SENSES

H.G. Wells. 'Men like Gods'. Cassell and Company, Ltd. 1923....................................... P67
Albert Einstein............................ P68
'The Ragged Trousered Philanthropists.' P353.Robert Tressell. 1914. Granada. 1965..... P69

WHY

RELATIVITY

Douglas Adams Hitchhikers Guide to the Galaxy............................ P75

DREAMS

'Everyman.' BBC1. TV. 12.11.85.   P76
The Bible. Genesis 37............................ P77
'Dreams That Come True.'David Ryback, Ph.D. & Letitia Sweitzer.
                                                        Diamond Books. 1988.   P78

OUT OF THE BODY

'Life After Life' Dr Raymond Moody.Jr MD. Corgi....................................... P80
'Closer to The Light.' P23. Melvin Morse MD with Paul Perry. Bantam Books. 1991..... P81
'Mindsight.' Kenneth Ring and Sharon Cooper. I Universe 2008............................ P81
William Gerhardi, 'Man Outside Himself.' P45 Prevost Battersby.
                                                        Psychic Book Club. 1943.... P82
'Gone West.' P160. J.S.M.Ward. BA Cambridge. Ryder. 1918............................ P82
You Cannot Die. P97.Ian Currie. Hamlyn. 1978............................ P82
Far Journeys. P296. Robert Monroe. Doubleday 1985............................ P83
'Journey of Souls.' P32 Llewellyn Publications. 1997............................ P83
'The Phenomena of Astral Projection.' P192 Muldoon & Carrington. Rider 1969........ P83
'Projections of the Consciousness.' Waldo Vieira. M. D
        International Institute of Projectiology& Conscientiology. 1997................ P84
px. Casebook of Astral Projection. Dr Robert Crookall. Citadel.1980........................... P85
Marlene Druhan. 'Naked Soul' P56 Llewellyn 1998............................ P85
Projections of the Consciousness P44/5. by Waldo Vieira.
        International Institute of Projectiology and Conscientiology. 1997............... P85
Oliver Fox Astral Projection. Rider. 1920............................ P86
Lew Sutton. 'Psychic News.' November 16th 1996............................ P86
'Man Outside Himself.' P90. Prevost Battersby. Psychic Book Club.1943.................... P87
'Man Outside Himself.' P93 Prevost Battersby. Psychic Book Club.1943.................... P88
Projections of the Consciousness. P70. Waldo Vieira, M.D. ASPR. SPR.
        International Institute for Projectiology and Conscientiology. (IIPC.) 1997........ P88
Out of the body experiences. P30 Robert Alvery. Regency Press. 1975........................... P88
Bruce Moen. 'Voyage beyond Doubt.' Hampton Roads............................ P88

THE FINAL OOBE

SURVIVAL THE EVIDENCE

GOD

GUIDANCE

VIRTUAL REALITY

WORDS ON THE PAGE

TIME

OF MANY LIVES

ETERNITY AND CONCLUSIONS.

THE SPIRITUAL LIFE. Michael Featherstone
2016, Amazon UK.

For many people in this modern world, life has no meaning; for them existence is empty, hollow and filled with pain: But there is far more to life than they realise. Like the song of the birds the soft and gentle voice of spirit often goes unnoticed; helping; guiding; informing and comforting each and every one of us. They are with us every day of our lives from the moment of birth, until we meet face to face once again, on the day that we return to our spiritual home.

I believe that the thoughts that follow have, to a greater or lesser extent, been given to me to share with those who will listen. I hope that you will find these ideas as interesting and inspiring as I do.

Do you think of God as a kind of Wizard of Oz; an old man in the sky that waved his magic wand to bring everything into existence? Do you believe that in some mysterious way he dishes out both bad and good luck seemingly at random and that *He* is amenable to persuasion? This collection of talks has been inspired by those that know at first hand the work that goes on behind the scenes. They tell us why life is so hard; why it often seems so unjust and what is more important, how to come to terms with more challenging experiences.

I have studied the evidence for Life after Death for over 40 years. 'The Spiritual Life' demonstrates the ministry of God through the work of countless spirit people many of whom have travelled with us on the path of eternity and know us better than we know ourselves. In the words of my inspirers this book is to, ...allow people to visualise; to come into the knowledge and to understand the simple message that God is everywhere always working.

Printed in Great Britain
by Amazon